LEARNING TO SAIL

★　　★　　★

LEARNING TO SAIL

THE ANNAPOLIS SAILING SCHOOL GUIDE FOR ALL AGES

★   ★   ★

By Di Goodman and Ian Brodie

With illustrations by Joan B. Machinchick

International Marine
Camden, Maine

For Russell, Seth, and Jessica

Published by International Marine®

10 9 8 7 6 5 4 3

Copyright © 1994 International Marine®, a division of The McGraw-Hill Companies.

Library of Congress Cataloging-in-Publication Data
Goodman, Di.
    Learning to sail : the Annapolis Sailing School guide for all ages / by Di Goodman and Ian Brodie ; with illustrations by Joan B. Machinchick.
        p.   cm.
    ISBN 0-07-024014-0 (alk. paper)
    1. Sailing. 2. Seamanship. I. Brodie, Ian. II. Machinchick, Joan B.
GV811.G66 1994
797.1'24--dc20   94-5643
                                                                              CIP

Questions regarding the content of this book should be addressed to:
International Marine
P.O. Box 220
Camden, ME 04843

Questions regarding the ordering of this book should be addressed to:
The McGraw-Hill Companies
Customer Service Department
P.O. Box 547
Blacklick, Ohio 43004
Retail Customers: 1-800-822-8158; Bookstores: 1-800-722-4726

Learning to Sail is printed on recycled paper containing a minimum of 50% total recycled fiber with 10% postconsumer de-inked fiber.

Printed by R.R. Donnelley, Crawfordsville, IN

Design by Ann Aspell

Production and page layout by Molly Mulhern

Edited by James R. Babb, Green Editorial, Pamela Benner, Matthew Eaton

CONTENTS

ACKNOWLEDGMENTS

We want to thank family members for being mentors, sounding boards, technical consultants, and psychological anchors as we endeavored to explain and illustrate the principles of sailing as simply and clearly as possible. Thanks also to: Jerry and Kathy Wood, Rick Franke and Tim Dowling, all of the Annapolis Sailing School; Brad Hill and the instructors and young sailors of the Cape St. Claire Yacht Club; staff of the Severn Sailing Association; Judith Hansen; Ron Turner and Gill Godwin of the Clacton Sailing Club in Essex, England; Jessica Mitchem; and the crew at International Marine, notably Jim Babb, Jon Eaton, and Pamela Benner.

INTRODUCTION

As Water Rat said in *The Wind in the Willows,* "Believe me, my young friend, there is *nothing*—absolutely nothing—half so much worth doing as simply messing about in boats."

How right he is! Hoisting your sails, riding the wind, heading off across the bay for a day of exploring, racing, or simply messing about . . . there really is nothing that can compare with the excitement, freedom, and sheer satisfaction of sailing.

Our goal is to help *you* learn to sail. We begin by learning about the boat—the names of its parts, how it's built, and how sails, rudders, and centerboards work. Then we learn how to rig a small sailboat and how to make it go where we want it to go, and do what we want it to do. We'll learn about safety, how to handle bad weather, and how to tie the simple knots that sailors have used for centuries.

And we remain true to sailing's traditions, using the language of the sea handed down from the days of Columbus, Magellan, and Drake. At first it may seem hard to remember that *port* is left, *starboard* is right, and a rope is actually a *line.* You may not have a clue just what a *clew* is . . . but you will.

And *we,* by the way, are Di Goodman, Ian Brodie, and Joan Machinchick. Di has been teaching beginners of all ages to sail for many years at the Annapolis Sailing School on the Chesapeake Bay. Ian is Washington correspondent for *The Times of London,* and Joan is a sailor and artist from Annapolis.

Di met Ian and his son Russell, then eleven, when they enrolled in her classes at the Annapolis Sailing School. When the Brodies returned home, they tried to find a sailing book written for young people that would refresh their memories about what they had learned. Unfortunately, most books about sailing seem to be a jumble of confusing details and theory that have been drained of any fun and adventure.

That's when the idea for this book was born. Together we created a basic book, using the proven instruction methods of the world's largest sailing school, to guide you through the theory and practice of sailing. We want to help you become a safe, capable, and confident sailor who understands what you and your boat are doing at all times.

We hope to fire your imaginations with the adventure of sailing. After all, who hasn't daydreamed of discovering new lands, rounding Cape Horn, or winning the America's Cup—even while steering the most humble dinghy into the dock?

So face forward, inboard hand on the tiller, and let's get started.

Good luck,
Di Goodman
Ian Brodie
Joan B. Machinchick

YOUR BOAT

We are going to learn how to sail.

To do it right, you have to know your boat inside and out. Play with it for a while. Touch and learn to use all its working parts. Be comfortable handling them. Before long, they should be as familiar to you as the furniture in your bedroom.

In this chapter you will find out how to rig your boat by fitting and raising the sails. At the end of the chapter there is a checklist to help you remember each step in the right order.

You will also learn some special words that sailors use. They are a little like a foreign language. To help you remember them, illustrations or definitions are given on the page where they first appear. Definitions for all of these words also are listed in the Glossary/Index at the end of the book.

There is a good reason for learning these words. If someone yells to you, "Grab that shackle!" you will know right away what they are talking about, without having to ask. Besides, it's quicker and more precise for the skipper to say, "Grab the main halyard shackle!" than to shout, "Grab that metal thing that looks like a little horseshoe at the end of the rope that hauls up that big sail!"

So, look out for the new words. They come from our nautical traditions. You will soon realize how useful they are.

In this chapter you'll learn a couple of nautical knots. On a sailboat, knots are used all the time. They are a challenge, but most of us get the hang of knots pretty quickly. Practice them ashore (even with your shoe-laces) until you can do them easily. And remember to untie them before you stand up.

There are five main parts to your sailboat, whether you have the smallest dinghy or a million-aire's yacht loaded with the latest gizmos. They are: 1. The

A shackle. To open and lock it, screw the pin crossing the open end of the U out or in. Most shackles are designed not to unscrew all the way so the pieces won't get separated.

body of the boat—the **hull**. 2. The **sails**, which use the wind to make it go. 3. The **mast**, which holds up the sails and which in turn is held upright by a set of wires called **shrouds** and **stays**. 4. The **rudder**, which steers the boat by means of a long handle called a **tiller**. 5. The **centerboard** or **keel**, which prevents the boat from slipping sideways under pressure from the wind.

The front of your boat is called the **bow**. Bows are pointed to cut down on drag as the boat goes through the water. The hull is sleek and streamlined, like a fish, for the same reason. Imagine how much water resistance there would be if you had a boat shaped like a box. The rear of your boat is the **stern**.

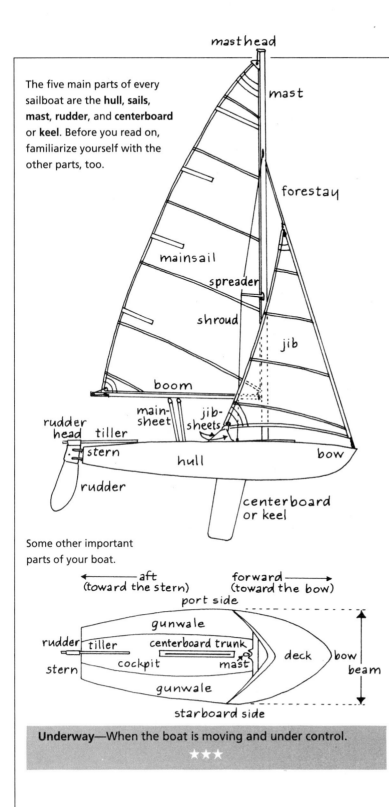

The five main parts of every sailboat are the **hull**, **sails**, **mast**, **rudder**, and **centerboard** or **keel**. Before you read on, familiarize yourself with the other parts, too.

masthead

mast

forestay

mainsail

spreader

shroud

jib

boom

main-sheet

jib-sheets

rudder head

tiller

stern

rudder

hull

bow

centerboard or keel

Some other important parts of your boat.

aft (toward the stern)

forward (toward the bow)

port side

gunwale

rudder

tiller

centerboard trunk

deck

bow

stern

cockpit

mast

beam

gunwale

starboard side

Underway—When the boat is moving and under control.

★★★

BALANCING THE BOAT

Right away you'll notice that your boat rolls or tips when you step on board. On all small boats, be sure to board near the middle of the **cockpit**, rather than onto a seat or the **gunwale**. The next thing you should do is lower the centerboard. This will add resistance under the water and help to keep the boat steady. Turn to page 16 for help lowering the centerboard.

Rocking is a part of a boat's natural movement in the water. You will develop strong "sea legs" as you grow skilled at keeping both yourself and the boat balanced properly. You'll probably find that it helps to squat or bend over so your weight is low when you move around on a bobbing boat. You'll also learn where to hang on. As you get moving, or **underway**, the boat will have the push of wind against the sail. This steadies the boat and reduces the amount of rocking back and forth.

SAILS AND MASTS

Although there are several kinds of sails and masts, this chapter describes the usual setup or **rig** on small, open sailboats, often called **dinghies**. Later you'll learn about other types of boats. They're fun to recognize when you're out on the water. For now, though, let's talk about small boats with two sails and one mast. The larger of these two sails is called the **mainsail**, and the smaller one is the **jib**.

When you look toward the bow of your boat, you're looking **forward**. When you look toward the back, or stern, you're looking **aft**. The jib is forward of the mast. The mainsail comes behind, or aft of, the mast.

PARTS OF THE SAIL

The usual shape for sails is a triangle. The forward edge of the sail is called the **luff**. The edge parallel to the deck is the **foot,** and the aft, sloping edge is the **leech**.

The top corner of the sail is called the **head**. The forward corner is the **tack**, and the aft corner is the **clew**.

The three unusual terms—luff, clew, and leech—came from European languages and date back to the times when Columbus sailed across the Atlantic. We have lots of modern equipment on our small boats today, but we owe our basic ideas about sailing to the hard-won wisdom of ancient mariners. Think about it. The wind and water haven't changed, just the way we use them.

Aft—Toward the stern or back of the boat.

Dinghy—Small open boat.

Forward—Toward the bow or front of a boat.

Rig—Setup of a boat's sails and spars.

★★★

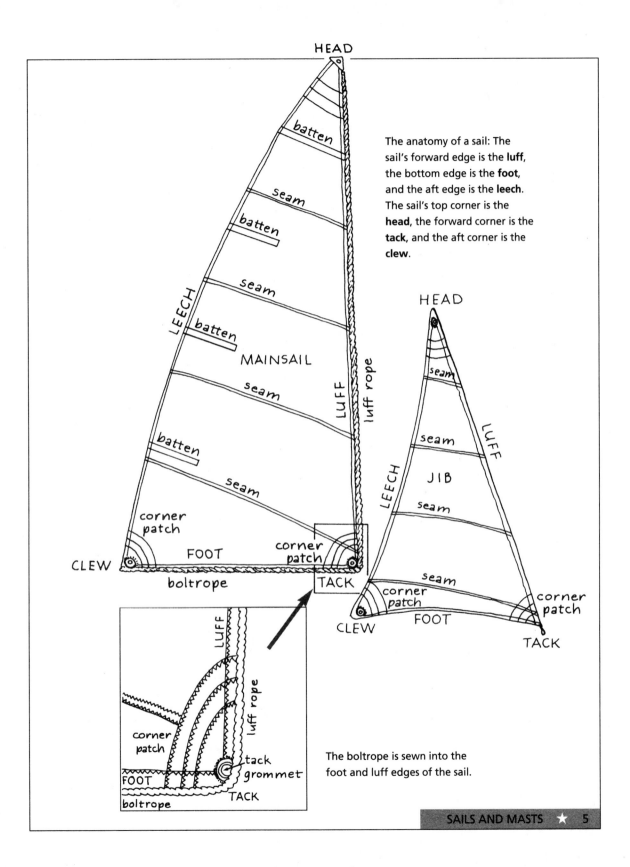

HEAD

batten

seam

batten

seam

LEECH

batten

MAINSAIL

seam

LUFF

luff rope

batten

seam

corner
patch

CLEW   FOOT   corner
patch

boltrope   TACK

The anatomy of a sail: The sail's forward edge is the **luff**, the bottom edge is the **foot**, and the aft edge is the **leech**. The sail's top corner is the **head**, the forward corner is the **tack**, and the aft corner is the **clew**.

HEAD

seam

seam

LEECH

JIB

LUFF

seam

seam

corner
patch

CLEW   FOOT   corner
patch

TACK

LUFF

luff rope

corner
patch

FOOT
TACK
boltrope

tack
grommet

The boltrope is sewn into the foot and luff edges of the sail.

RIGGING

FIRST THE MAINSAIL

Let's put sails on your boat. This is often called **bending on.** It means you attach the sails to the mast and to the **boom**, which swings out from the mast and holds the foot of the mainsail. The boom is held to the mast by a metal hinge that can wiggle like a goose's neck, and it is called a **gooseneck**.

You want the bow pointing into the wind so the sail **luffs** when raised, keeping the boat from sailing away. It is best to bend on the sails with your boat tied up by the bow to the dock or **mooring** so your sails will flap without catching the wind until you want them to.

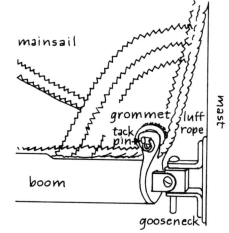

The O-shaped grommet in the tack corner of the sail is secured with a tack pin at the forward end of the boom.

1. Slide the boltrope into the groove along the top of the boom.

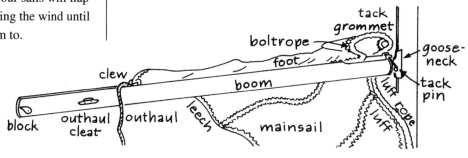

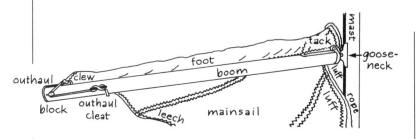

2. Then draw the clew toward the stern by pulling on the outhaul until the foot is tight and make it fast to the outhaul cleat.

Bend On—To fasten sails to a boat.

Loose-footed—Sail secured to boom only at the tack and clew.

Luff—(1) Forward edge of a triangular sail. (2) Rippling or flapping at the forward edge of a sail.

Mooring—An anchored float to tie up to.

★★★

Start by unpacking the mainsail from its bag and piling it into the cockpit so you can slide its bottom edge, or foot, into the groove on top of the boom. Run your hands along the foot of the sail and you will feel a braided rope sewn into the edge. This is called a **boltrope**.

The boltrope runs the length of the foot of the sail from the clew corner to the tack corner, and sometimes up the luff to the head of the mainsail. At the tack corner you will find a metal ring, known as a **grommet**, sewn into your sail.

At the clew corner of the mainsail there's a short rope, often tied to another grommet, called the **outhaul.**

To fit the sail onto the boom, start by sliding the clew end of the boltrope into the open groove on the boom.

By pulling on the outhaul tied to the clew, you can guide the boltrope aft all the way along the boom until the grommet at the tack corner is lined up with the forward end of the boom. Fasten this grommet to the fitting on the boom with a shackle or with a metal peg called a **tack pin.** If there is no groove in the top of the boom, your sail may be **loose-footed** and will fasten to the boom only at the corners.

Now go back to the aft end of the boom, where you will find a pulley or **block**. Pass the outhaul around the block and pull to snug the foot of the sail tight along the boom.

How much should you pull on the outhaul? Just enough to stretch the sail tight without puckering. When you pull your T-shirt in two directions over your stomach, it wrinkles. That's too tight. If your sail puckers, **ease off** (let out) the outhaul just enough to make it flat.

When the sail is tight enough, **make fast** the outhaul to the boom with a **cleat hitch**. You tie it around a **horn cleat** on the aft end of the boom. (Sheets are not secured with a cleat hitch so that they can be let go quickly. Instead, they sometimes have special cleats with quick-release mechanisms.)

Here is a pun that will help you remember to fasten the tack corner before you tie down the clew: "If I tack it down first, I'll have a clew what to do next."

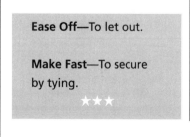

Ease Off—To let out.

Make Fast—To secure by tying.
★★★

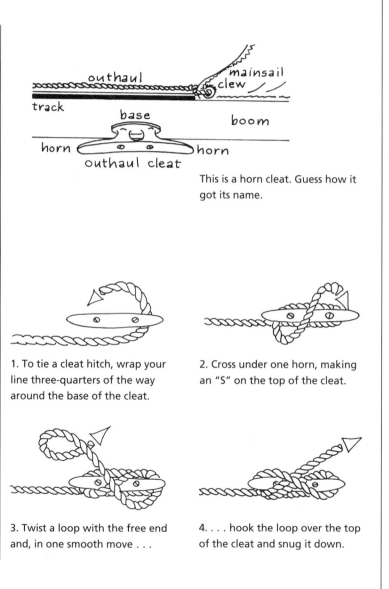

This is a horn cleat. Guess how it got its name.

1. To tie a cleat hitch, wrap your line three-quarters of the way around the base of the cleat.

2. Cross under one horn, making an "S" on the top of the cleat.

3. Twist a loop with the free end and, in one smooth move . . .

4. . . . hook the loop over the top of the cleat and snug it down.

Aloft—Up.

Halyard—Line used to hoist sails.

Line—Rope, to sailors.

Port—Left side of a boat when you are looking forward.

Starboard—Right side of a boat when you are looking forward.

Stow—To put away.

★ ★ ★

Tying the cleat hitch takes a little practice, but it's worth the effort. When you do it right, it will not jam, which is important and especially useful when you need to untie it quickly.

Now that you have secured the foot of the sail to the boom, you are ready to attach its forward, or luff, edge to the mast and haul it up.

The rope, or **line,** that pulls your mainsail to the top of the mast is a **halyard**. You will find the mainsail halyard on the right, or **starboard,** side of the mast as you face forward. When not sailing, the loose end of the halyard should be **stowed** on its horn cleat near the bottom of the mast, and the shackled end attached to any nearby fitting.

The halyard is a line twice as long as the mast. It starts at the bottom and goes up to the top of the mast (this half is often wire-rope) and runs back down again to you.

If you have external halyards, you will be able to see both halves dangling down from the masthead. Holding the ends in your hands, you can feel that if you pull down on one end the other end goes up. (If you have internal halyards, half of the halyard runs up inside the mast, and you must pull it out from a hole near the boom.)

Be careful: Do not let go with either hand, because if half of the halyard gets pulled up to the top of the mast you may need help getting it back down again. Every sailor has done this at least once, but none of them will talk about it.

Next, look **aloft** to the top of the mast to make certain your halyard has no tangles that would prevent it from moving smoothly.

One end of your halyard will have a shackle on it. To start raising the mainsail, you need to clip this shackle to the grommet at the head of the sail. Then gradually pull down on the

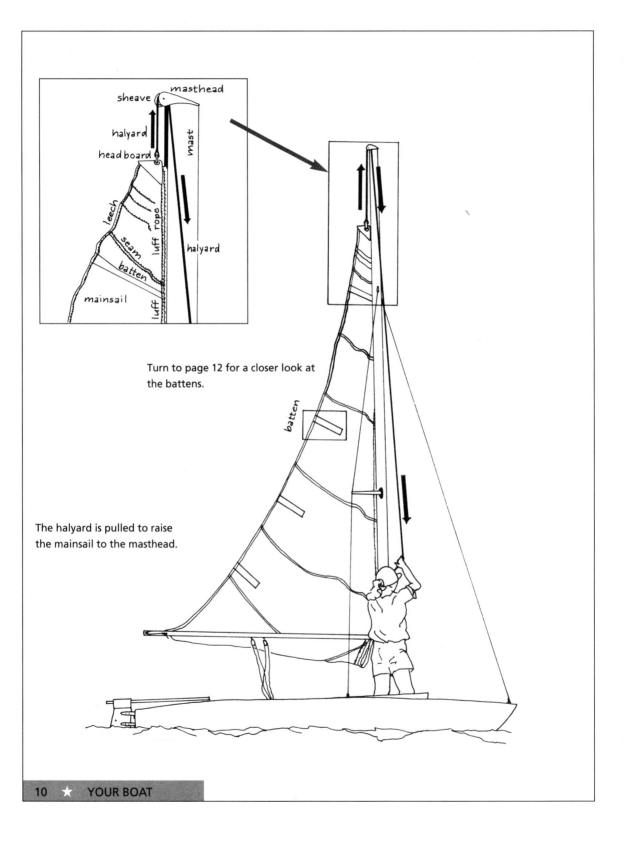

masthead

sheave

halyard

headboard

mast

halyard

leech

luff rope

seam

batten

mainsail

luff

Turn to page 12 for a closer look at the battens.

batten

The halyard is pulled to raise the mainsail to the masthead.

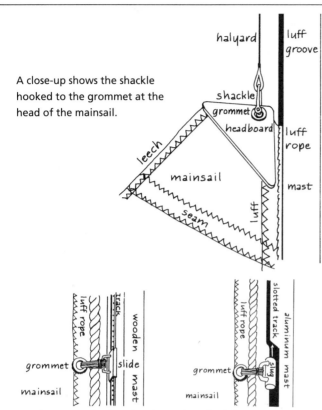

A close-up shows the shackle hooked to the grommet at the head of the mainsail.

halyard
luff groove
shackle
grommet
headboard
luff rope
mast
leech
mainsail
seam
luff

luff rope
track
wooden mast
grommet
slide
mainsail

luff rope
slotted track
aluminum mast
grommet
slug
mainsail

Some boats may be fitted with a sail track. Slides are sewn to the mainsail that fit in the track. As the halyard if pulled, these slides (or slugs) move up and down.

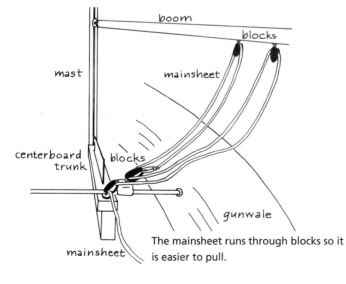

boom
blocks
mast
mainsheet
centerboard trunk
blocks
gunwale
mainsheet

The mainsheet runs through blocks so it is easier to pull.

halyard as you feed the luff edge of the sail up into the track on the mast. (Your luff edge may have a cord, and feed into a slot in the mast like a boltrope; it may have plastic cylinders; or it may have metal slides that run up a track.)

Pull on the halyard until the mainsail is all the way up the mast. If your sail fits properly, its luff should stretch out nice and tight just before the head of the sail reaches the top of the mast. Be sure the luff is tight but flat, not puckered. Wrap the halyard around the horn cleat on the starboard side of the mast (see drawing on page 12). Then secure it with a cleat hitch and coil the rest of the halyard, looping it neatly over the starboard cleat so that no one trips over it. Check to be sure your **mainsheet** is loose. While you're in port, you want to let the sail flap in the breeze. We'll talk more about the mainsheet in chapter 4.

Stand back and admire your ready mainsail.

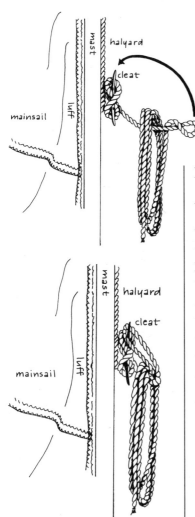

Coil and hang the end of the main halyard neatly on the starboard cleat.

BATTENS

With sails up and flapping, look at your mainsail again. Spaced along its leech edge and running parallel to the boom you may find two or three long, horizontal strips of fiberglass or wood. These are **battens**, and they fit into pockets sewn into the sail. They stiffen the leech edge and flatten the sail. The pockets may be sewn shut, so you need to be very careful when stowing the sail at the end of the day. If the battens are removable, slide them out and stow them separately. Smaller boats do not always have battens, but they are a big help in giving a good shape to your sail when you are underway.

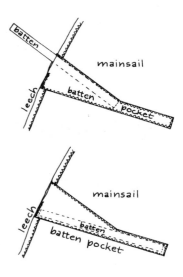

Many jibs are equipped with jib hanks to secure the sail's luff to the forestay.

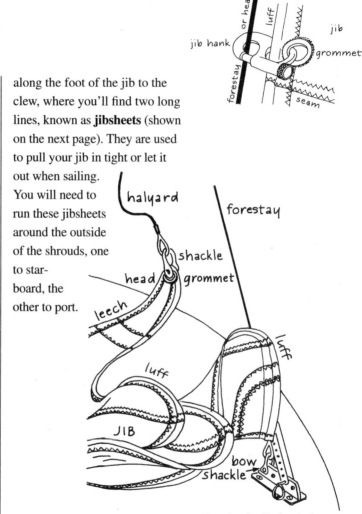

NOW THE JIB

The three corners and edges of the jib have the same names as those on the mainsail. Find the narrowest corner, and that will be the head. Run your hand down along the luff to the foot. The luff may have **jib hanks** sewn along it to snap onto the **forestay**, so you can easily tell it from the leech. At the forward corner of the foot, the tack, there will usually be a sailmaker's label and, more important, there will be a grommet. Hook this grommet to a shackle, which you should find fixed to the bow of your boat. Then snap the jib hanks onto the forestay, working from the foot to the head (some jibs with wire luffs have no jib hanks). You may have a cable on the luff that is independent of the forestay and pulls very tight. The different luff configurations all serve the purpose of creating a stiff forward edge.

Next, run your hand back along the foot of the jib to the clew, where you'll find two long lines, known as **jibsheets** (shown on the next page). They are used to pull your jib in tight or let it out when sailing. You will need to run these jibsheets around the outside of the shrouds, one to starboard, the other to port.

To raise the jib, hook the grommet at the tack corner onto the bow shackle. Snap the jib hanks onto the forestay. Shackle the jib halyard to the head of the jib and haul down on the halyard until the jib is tight. Cleat it to port.

You will find a metal or plastic ring mounted on each side of the deck. These are called **fairleads**. Some boats have a small block to lead the jibsheets. Feed your jibsheets through the fairleads and back into the cockpit. To stop the sheets from running back out through the fairleads when the wind fills the jib, tie a **stopper knot,** which looks like a figure eight, in the end of each jibsheet. Don't pull in or cleat your jibsheets while in port. Let the jib flap just like the mainsail.

Finally, locate your jib halyard. One end will be cleated on the port side of the mast; the other end will have a shackle. Attach this shackle to the head of the jib. Uncleat the other end and hoist the jib. The jib may not go all the way to the top of the mast, but you need to be certain it is tight enough not to sag when it fills with wind. Cleat, coil, and hang the jib halyard on the port side of the

mast, just as you did with the main halyard to starboard. Check again and make sure your jibsheets are free while you are tied up. Your jibsheets are going to flap around like crazy until you are under sail. That's what they should do.

The jibsheets, one port and one starboard, run back to the cockpit, around the outside of the shrouds, and through the plastic rings known as fairleads. The ends are knotted to stop them from slipping back out of the fairleads.

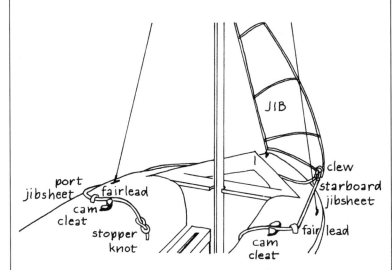

To make a stopper knot, hang the end of the jibsheet over your hand.

Take the loose end and wind it once all the way around itself, forming an 8.

Pull the loose end through the top loop. This knot should be about one hand's width away from the end of the jibsheet.

CLEATS

There may be at least four kinds of cleats on your boat. As you have seen, horn cleats are for tying a cleat hitch. You will see them on docks and pilings, too.

The other three are **jam**, **cam**, and **clam** cleats. They are all used to secure sheets. The jam cleat is very similar to the horn cleat, except that one end is pinched in and bites the line you wrap around it. The cam cleat has two spring-loaded jaws that hold the line as you pull it through them. The clam cleat has ridges like a clam shell. When you put a line in from the top, the ridges prevent it from slipping.

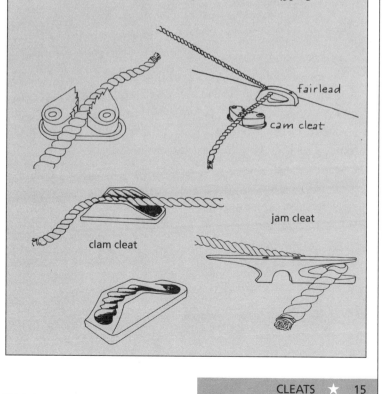

fairlead

cam cleat

clam cleat

jam cleat

RUDDERS, CENTERBOARDS, AND DAGGER-BOARDS

You may need to install the **rudder** and **tiller** at this point. Usually the rudder has a long bolt that slides into a socket mounted on the boat, like a bolt on a door. Probably there will be a mechanism that sounds a good click when the rudder is properly set in place. The tiller, if it's not attached already, may slide into a coupling on the rudder's head and lock in place with an elastic cord.

The centerboard on small boats is a sheet of thin wood, fiberglass, or metal. It fits in a long slot with raised sides, called the **centerboard trunk,** in the middle of the boat. You can lower and raise the centerboard by a line, called a **pennant,** that is cleated on the trunk. The centerboard pivots on a bolt at its forward end. As mentioned earlier, you should lower the centerboard when you first get in the boat.

A **daggerboard** is just another kind of centerboard.

Instead of pivoting, it slides up and down through a slot in the hull, like a dagger in a sheath.

You can use a stretchy line called a **bungee cord** as a safety line to keep the centerboard or daggerboard in place. They should be secured before setting off. The bungee may go over the top of your daggerboard to hold it down or pull tight and catch in a slot to hold the centerboard in place.

When the wind is directly behind the boat, you can pull up the centerboard to reduce friction and go slightly faster.

The job of a centerboard or daggerboard is to prevent the boat from sliding sideways when the wind is blowing across the side of the boat. Some boats have fixed keels that serve the same purpose.

If the boat **capsizes,** as discussed in chapter 8, you will right it by standing on the centerboard. That's why you make sure it's locked in place.

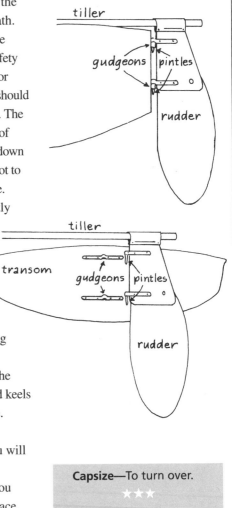

Capsize—To turn over.
★★★

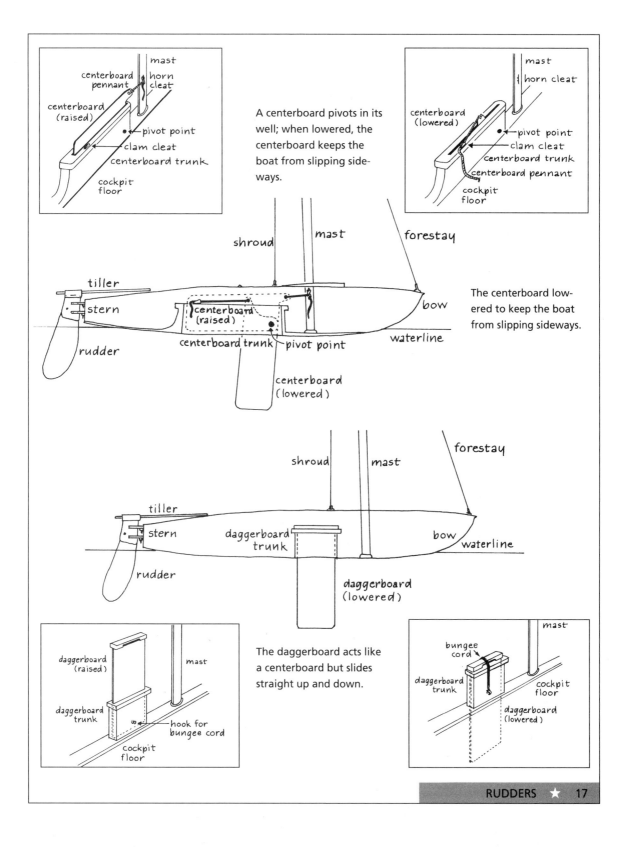

centerboard
pennant
mast
horn
cleat
centerboard
(raised)
pivot point
clam cleat
centerboard trunk
cockpit
floor

A centerboard pivots in its well; when lowered, the centerboard keeps the boat from slipping sideways.

mast
horn cleat
centerboard
(lowered)
pivot point
clam cleat
centerboard trunk
centerboard pennant
cockpit
floor

shroud
mast
forestay

tiller
stern
centerboard
(raised)
bow
rudder
centerboard trunk
pivot point
waterline
centerboard
(lowered)

The centerboard lowered to keep the boat from slipping sideways.

forestay
shroud
mast

tiller
stern
daggerboard
trunk
bow
waterline
rudder
daggerboard
(lowered)

daggerboard
(raised)
mast
daggerboard
trunk
hook for
bungee cord
cockpit
floor

The daggerboard acts like a centerboard but slides straight up and down.

mast
bungee
cord
daggerboard
trunk
cockpit
floor
daggerboard
(lowered)

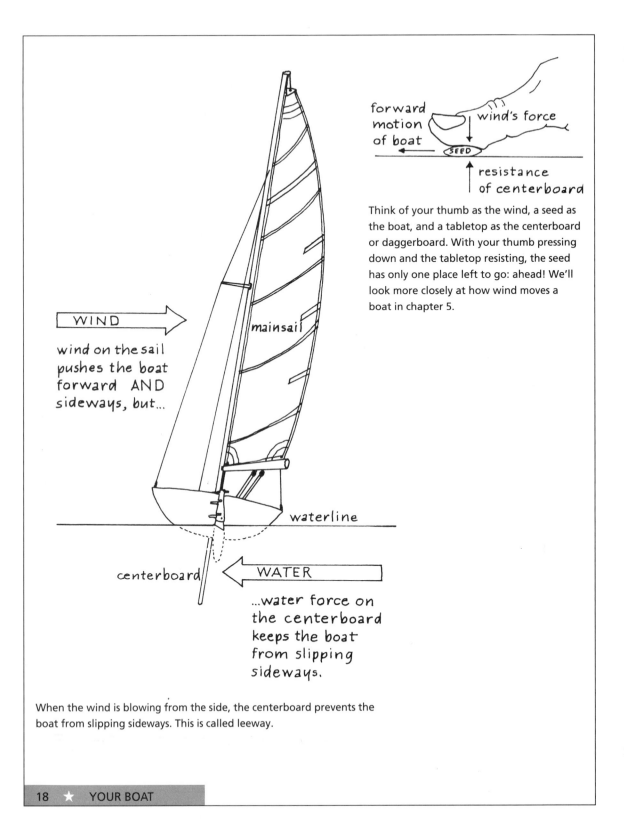

forward
motion
of boat

wind's force

SEED

resistance
of centerboard

Think of your thumb as the wind, a seed as
the boat, and a tabletop as the centerboard
or daggerboard. With your thumb pressing
down and the tabletop resisting, the seed
has only one place left to go: ahead! We'll
look more closely at how wind moves a
boat in chapter 5.

WIND

wind on the sail
pushes the boat
forward AND
sideways, but...

mainsail

waterline

centerboard

WATER

...water force on
the centerboard
keeps the boat
from slipping
sideways.

When the wind is blowing from the side, the centerboard prevents the
boat from slipping sideways. This is called leeway.

RIGGING CHECKLIST

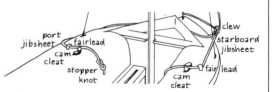

You're almost ready to set sail. But first let's run through the rigging checklist.

- Find where the wind is coming from and make sure your bow points into it. If your boat is tied to a mooring or dock, it will automatically try to point, or head, into the wind.
- Drop the centerboard and secure it.
- Stow personal gear.
- Fit the mainsail first. The main halyard is on the starboard side.
- Fit the foot of the mainsail from the clew to the tack by sliding the boltrope or sail slides into the boom track. Secure the tack with a tack pin or shackle and cleat-hitch the outhaul to make fast the clew.

- Clear the halyard aloft so that it runs freely before attaching the shackle to the head of the sail.

- Uncleat the mainsheet and just let it hang for now.
- Feed hand over hand down the luff to be sure the head of the sail is not twisted. Fit the luff edge of the mainsail by inserting the boltrope or slides into the mast track from head to foot.

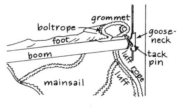

- Raise the mainsail to the top of the mast and cleat the halyard to starboard with a cleat hitch.
- Move forward with the jib and attach the tack to the shackle on the bow. Snap jib hanks on

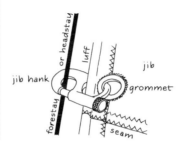

the forestay.
- Run the jibsheets port and starboard outside the shrouds into the cockpit through the fairlead blocks or rings. Put a stopper knot in each end.
- Attach the halyard shackle to the jib head for raising. Stand aft of the mast while you raise the jib (those jibsheets can be wild).
- Hoist the jib. Get the halyard tight and cleat it to port.
- Drop the rudder, if it's folded back.
- Check your safety equipment (see chapter 2).

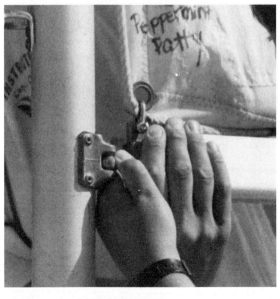

Hoisting the mainsail for the first time can be easier on dry land. Here (top left), the halyard is shackled to the grommet at the mainsail's head; and (top right) the halyard is raised slowly while the mainsail's luff is fed into the mast track. At left, the mainsail's tack is shackled to the tack fitting on the gooseneck.

SAFE AND SOUND

Sailing safely is not just important, it's absolutely essential.

Not only that, but *you* are in charge of making your boat safe.

As skipper, you are in charge of *everything* about your boat. That means your own safety and the safety of everyone sailing with you. *You* are responsible once you sail away.

This is not meant to scare you, but to encourage you to be prepared in case you run into a tough situation.

Make sure you have emergency equipment on board every time you set sail. There is a safety checklist at the end of this chapter. Memorize it, and always run through it before you set out.

There is also a section in this chapter on the proper clothing for sailing. Deciding what to wear, and what extra clothing to take, is part of being safe and sound. It ruins the fun of sailing if you get caught in a heavy downpour without rain gear or by a cold wind without a windbreaker.

SAFETY FIRST

There are four important ways to ensure your own safety even before you set foot on your boat.

- Let someone know where you're going and when you'll be back. Then, when you're back ashore, let that person know.
- Listen to local weather forecasts on the radio. Don't sail if a storm is coming. (You'll learn how to handle unexpected bad weather and other mishaps in chapter 8.)
- If you are sailing somewhere by yourself, be certain you first have the approval of a parent or sailing instructor who knows you.
- Know your waters. There may be regulations and special things to know, sometimes called *local knowledge,* that are just about your area. Local knowledge can help with things like aids to navigation, strong currents, or rocks. Ask an experienced local sailor if there are any special rules or conditions where you sail.

Even if your state doesn't require that you pass a small-craft safety course, it's smart to take one. Courses are given regularly by the Coast Guard Auxiliary, state boating commissions, and many yacht clubs. Ask around, or check the Yellow Pages of your telephone book, under Boating Instruction.

WHAT TO TAKE

Here are the safety items you will need:

- **Life jackets:** You are required by the Coast Guard to carry one "personal flotation device," or PFD, for each person on board. PFDs must always be within easy reach. The Coast Guard and many other experts recommend that small-boat sailors wear their jackets at all times.

This is a good idea. In some states it is the law.

At the Annapolis Sailing School, all nonswimmers *must* wear life jackets on training boats. Nonswimmers are those who cannot swim at least 30 yards, even with rest stops for treading water or floating on their backs.

You can choose among three types of life jackets:

Type I, an offshore life jacket that will turn an unconscious person face up in the water.

Type II, a near-shore life vest that is more comfortable but won't always turn an unconscious person right side up.

Type III, a life jacket similar to Type II, designed so wearers can turn themselves face up.

Of these three, the Type II life vest is a good choice for the level of small-boat sailing described in this book.

You should also carry a throwable, buoyant cushion or ring known as a **Type IV** device.

Make sure you are within the weight restriction (shown on the label) of your life jacket, even after lunch.

- **Lines:** It's a good idea to have two extra lengths of line on board for docking or for use as backup or replacement for the rigging.

Have one short, thin line of several feet and a longer one of 15 to 20 feet. The longer line may help if there is a person in

This is a Type II life vest, which you should wear at all times.

the water. Although you must throw a ring or life jacket immediately to anyone who falls overboard and then turn around to get them, the line may help bring them on board.

- **Whistle:** The Coast Guard says all vessels must have on board some effective means of making noise—that is, other than your voice. A whistle tied to your life jacket works well.

• **Bailer:** A small dinghy is unlikely to have an automatic system for emptying any water that comes in. It's not dangerous to have a little water in the bottom of your boat. But when there is enough to fill a one-gallon plastic milk bottle, you need to **bail**.

Cut the bottom out of such a bottle or a large, plastic laundry detergent container. Leave the top screwed on, and you have a perfect scoop for bailing.

A 1-gallon milk bottle with the bottom cut out makes an ideal bailer. Secure it with a light line so you won't lose it overboard.

Tie the bottle's handle with a long, thin line down low to the mast. This will prevent your bailer from being lost overboard.

• **Paddle:** It's only common sense to have another way of getting back to shore in case the wind dies or you have some other difficulty with your sails. So take a paddle.

There are several kinds of small, folding paddles that will do just fine. You need to stow your paddle out of the way. Maybe you can lash it to the centerboard trunk. An even better idea is to use sticky-backed Velcro pads, available from hardware stores. Put two pads on the side of the cockpit, line them up with two more on the paddle, and the paddle will cling there like a barnacle.

• **Tools:** Take on board a small canvas or plastic bag carrying a few tools and spare parts. You need just enough to cover emergencies: a screwdriver, a

pair of pliers, an extra tack pin, and an extra shackle. A roll of silver duct tape and a ball of tarred twine called **marline** are also useful to have aboard in a pinch.

The bag should also contain a **rigging knife**, preferably one with a **marlinspike** to loosen knots and shackles.

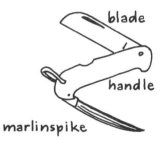

• **First aid:** The tool bag should also have a small first-aid kit of the kind you can buy in drugstores. It should contain

Marline—Tarred twine.

★★★

Danforth anchor.

shackle

shank

flukes

stock

crown

Band-Aids, anti-infection ointment for cuts, even meat tenderizer for jellyfish stings if you sail in warmer ocean waters. Ask an experienced sailor how to use these emergency items in advance, just in case.

• **Sunscreen:** Doctors and scientists today agree that sunburn is harmful to human skin. Even if the day is cloudy, you can get burned. So take with you and *use* sunscreen lotion that is waterproof and has a Sun Protection Factor (SPF) of 20 to 30, especially if you burn easily. Put double doses on lips and nose. If you go swimming, remember that a lotion's waterproof protection falls by 40 percent after 20 minutes in the water. Make sure you take *lotion*, not oil, which leaves a slippery film that can make your deck and cockpit treacherous.

• **Wristwatch:** It's important to know the time so that you can

turn for home early enough to be back for lunch, or by the tide's turn, or well before sundown—or when you promised.

• **Water bottle:** When you spend a day outdoors, your body needs water. Sodas and other sugary drinks are not great for quenching thirst. Take water in a plastic, not glass, bottle. Or fill a plastic jug that has a lid with ice and a little water. As the ice melts, you'll have a cold drink.

• **Anchor:** You should carry an **anchor** with an anchor line attached to it for anything more than sailing just off shore.

In an open dinghy, it is difficult to find a safe place to keep an anchor where it will not slide around and get in the way. The best idea is to lash it to the foot of the mast.

The anchor line—called an **anchor rode**—should be neatly coiled and looped over the stem, or shank, of the

anchor. For 10 to 15 feet of water depth you need no more than 100 feet of lightweight line. Polypropylene line is kind of annoying because it is scratchy, but it is light and strong.

• **Compass:** See the sidebar and drawing on page 26.

That's our list of safety equipment. If you take these items with you every time, they will give you added confidence. Some of them will make it easier for you to handle a difficult situation without panicking.

Above all, you must take your own safety seriously. You should not risk your life, or the lives of others, by allowing anyone on board who is under the influence of alcohol or drugs. They face an increased danger of drowning if they fall in unexpectedly. Be smart and respect the potential dangers.

Bearing—The direction of one object from another, measured in degrees from north, or measured relative to the boat's center-line.

★★★

YOUR COMPASS

As a day sailor, you can usually figure out your location by checking landmarks on the shore. But what happens if you're out of sight of land, or a thick fog suddenly rolls in? That's when you need your hand-held compass.

As you know, a compass has an arrow that points to magnetic north. Try this experiment on dry land: Stand facing north with the compass in your hand. Now turn to the right. The arrow continues pointing north, but the dial tells you that you're facing east at 90 degrees. You have just taken a simple **bearing**. It's the same on a boat. As you face the bow, compass in hand, it will show you your bearing, or direction.

You must have a working knowledge of direction, just as you must for the weather. Smart sailors always keep in mind which way is north. It gives you a fix on where the shore is. So even when you can't see land, you can still check your compass and head for home.

It's usually cooler out on the water than on land, so be prepared, even in the middle of summer, with a light jacket or long-sleeved shirt. Take a warmer jacket or wool sweater for early spring and late fall.

Wetsuits are popular as protection from wind and spray in areas where the water rarely gets warm. They are made from thick, rubbery material that allows just a little water between your skin and the suit. Your body heats up the water, which acts as a layer of insulation and keeps out the cold.

Denim or canvas shorts are best because they don't get caught easily on sharp edges.

If it's really warm, you'll want to wear a bathing suit for swimming. But out of the water wear shorts over the suit to protect you from the pinch of cleats, winches, and other hardware that may be mounted where you want to sit.

If there's a chance of rain,

take your **foul-weather gear** in a waterproof gym bag. You can find inexpensive sets of waterproof jacket and pants at surplus stores. The plastic ones are excellent for keeping you dry and protecting you from the wind.

To help cut down on the glare in bright sunshine, a wide-brimmed hat or baseball cap is recommended. In foul weather, a baseball cap will keep rain out of your eyes, especially important if you wear glasses.

Sunglasses are a personal choice, but many sailors wear them. The water's reflected glare makes the light brighter than on land. Look for sunglasses that filter out ultraviolet light, which can burn your eyes. Sunglasses or prescription glasses can be among the most expensive pieces of hardware on board. To be sure to keep them safe, wear a neck strap.

Many people like to wear leather deck shoes, but this footwear is better suited for walking around the deck of a cruise ship. On your boat, your feet are going to be sloshing around in water. Wet leather shoes are stiff, uncomfortable, and dye your feet orange. It's better to wear sandals with Velcro straps that will dry quickly in the air. Or wear sneakers that you don't mind getting wet.

Check the tread on your shoes to be certain they aren't slippery. Look for a sole that will stick to a wet surface. The best soles often have tiny slits in a zigzag pattern. There are many such sneakers, with nonskid soles and canvas uppers, made just for boating.

Running shoes or athletic shoes with black soles can leave marks on the deck. (But if you have a black deck, no problem!)

Don't wear rings, bracelets, long earrings, and necklaces while sailing. Not only is there a chance of losing these items overboard, but they can cause accidents if they get caught in the rigging or other equipment.

Holding on to lines can be tough on your hands, especially in cool weather, so gloves can be useful. Sailing gloves usually have the fingertips cut out so you can still tie knots. Even gardening gloves will help you keep a good grip on your lines.

SAFETY CHECKLIST

- Have you told someone where you're going and when you intend to return? Have you checked the local weather forecast?
- Life jackets for everyone on board, plus a throwable cushion or ring
- Two extra lengths of line, one short, one long
- Whistle
- Bailer
- Paddle
- Tool bag with screwdriver, pliers, tack pin, shackle, rigging knife or scissors, marline
- First-aid kit
- Sunscreen
- Wristwatch
- Water bottle
- Anchor, if you are going for several hours or you won't be close to shore
- Compass

SEASICKNESS

Seasickness affects many people to varying degrees—even sailors with years of experience. The queasy feeling is brought on by rough water, ranging from a big swell to choppy waves hitting the boat broadside. The swaying and pitching sets off alarm signals to the brain from minute organs in the inner ears. Seasickness causes nausea, dizziness, and sometimes vomiting.

Various remedies can be taken beforehand. Over-the-counter pills should be taken with extreme care because they can cause drowsiness. Some people find special wrist bands effective. There are also stick-on patches you wear on the skin behind one ear, but they require a doctor's prescription. Sometimes what we think is seasickness is dehydration; drinking plenty of water can help.

You can often avoid seasickness by staying busy. A spell at the tiller can keep your mind off feeling queasy. Cast your eyes on the distant horizon rather than the whitecaps close at hand. If you are on a boat with a cabin, do not go below deck to lie down; with no land or horizon to focus your eyes on, you will only feel worse. Try to head for calmer water.

HANDLE

UNDERWAY

Now the adventure begins. You've rigged your boat. You have all the safety equipment aboard. Now we're going to figure out how to make the boat go. This is called getting **underway**.

Underway—When the boat is moving and under control.
★★★

FINDING THE WIND

As sailors, we look at the world in a new way—always checking where the wind is coming from and how hard it's blowing.

You can't see the wind, but you can see what it does to trees, smoke from chimneys, your hair, and hats. Just look at how a flag blows away from the wind.

You can also feel the wind. One way is to wet your finger and hold it up in the air. The side of your finger closest to the wind will get cool first. Birds always perch facing into the wind so the breeze doesn't ruffle their feathers.

You will also see the wind as it comes across the water, causing ripples that make the surface look darker.

You'll eventually be able to tell the direction of the wind without thinking about it, just from the way it blows on your cheeks or through your hair. It becomes a habit: longtime

sailors always check where the wind is coming from, even on dry land.

On sailboats, you can check the wind direction from **telltales**, strips of wool or yarn tied high up on the shrouds. These yarns flutter in the wind and show you where the wind is coming from, no matter where the boat is headed. Red ones are the easiest to see.

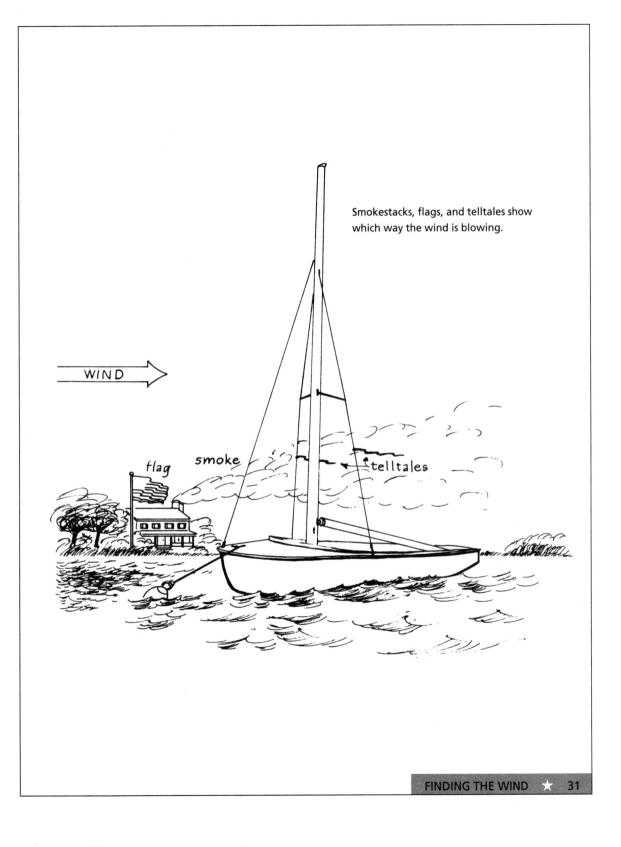

Smokestacks, flags, and telltales show which way the wind is blowing.

WIND

flag

smoke

telltales

PREPARING TO LEAVE THE DOCK

Normally, your boat is tied by its bow to the dock or a mooring, so it also hangs away from the wind, like a gigantic telltale.

When the wind is blowing head on to the bow like this, your boat is in the **no-sail zone**. As long as the boat faces the wind in the no-sail zone, and the mainsheet and jibsheet are loose, the wind can't push against one side of the sail and make the boat move, although it will pull impatiently from side to side against the mooring, just to let you know it's ready to go. You can raise the sails without worrying about your boat sailing away.

Think of the no-sail zone in another way. Imagine an apple pie. If you take a slice of pie for yourself and another slice for your crewmember, you'll have an empty space in the pie pan that is about a quarter of the circle. If the wind is blowing down the middle of that empty space, and your bow points directly into it, your sails will flap noisily in the breeze. Remember from chapter 1, this is called luffing. But your sails will not fill, and you'll be going nowhere. Where there is pie remaining in the pan, you can sail. The no-sail zone is where the pan is empty. We will keep going over this in different ways, but keep that picture in mind.

It is only in the no-sail zone that we raise or lower sails. Once we turn the bow so that the wind can blow on just one side of the sails, or **fall off** the wind (see the drawing on page 34), the boat will tug at its mooring to get underway, like a dog straining on a leash. Go back to the apple pie. If your bow is pointed at the empty spot where you took your piece, falling off the wind is moving from there to pointing at a piece of remaining pie.

A quick way to figure out which side of your boat the wind is coming over is to check the boom. It always hangs on the side of the boat away from the wind. The wind pushes it there.

Fall Off—To move the bow away from the wind.

★★★

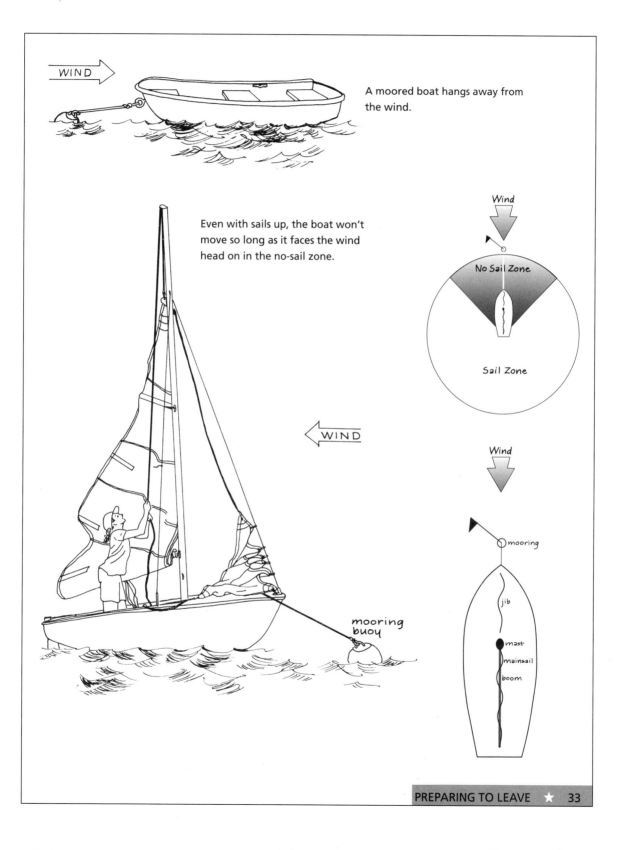

WIND →

A moored boat hangs away from the wind.

Even with sails up, the boat won't move so long as it faces the wind head on in the no-sail zone.

← WIND

Wind

No Sail Zone

Sail Zone

Wind

mooring

jib

mast

mainsail

boom

mooring buoy

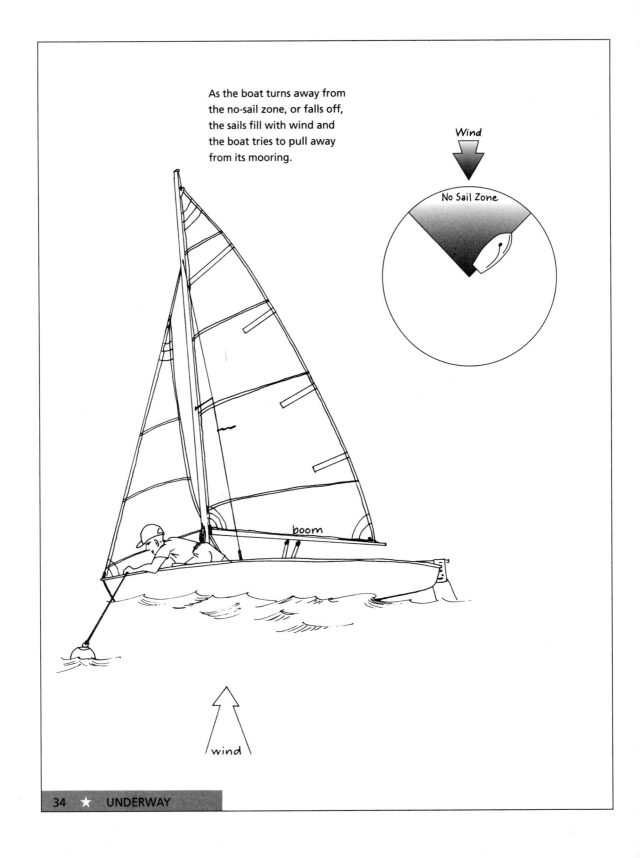

As the boat turns away from the no-sail zone, or falls off, the sails fill with wind and the boat tries to pull away from its mooring.

Wind

No Sail Zone

boom

wind

FINDING THE CORRECT TACK

On boats with no engine, you need to raise both sails all the way, so you're fully prepared to sail, before you untie from the mooring.

Before you untie, or **cast off**, stop, look at boats, wind, docks, and rocks nearby, and figure out a path that will let you leave the mooring without banging into anything. When sailors talk about the direction of the wind on their sails, they are referring to the **tack** they are on. You must choose which tack gives you the most room to get by.

If the wind is coming over the starboard side of the boat, you are on a starboard tack. When the wind is from the port side, it puts you on a port tack.

If the wind blows head on over the bow, the sails are in the center and luffing because you are in the no-sail zone.

The side the wind is coming from is called the **windward** side. The side away from the wind is called the **leeward** side.

The boom and the sails are on the leeward side—keep in mind that the wind pushes them away.

Cast Off—To untie from a dock or mooring.
★ ★ ★

The wind blows from the windward side to the leeward side of the boat. The wind puts the boom on the leeward side.

leeward

WIND

windward

When the wind comes from right to left, it blows over the starboard side of the boat and pushes the sails to port. When the wind comes from left to right, it blows over the port side, pushing the sails to starboard.

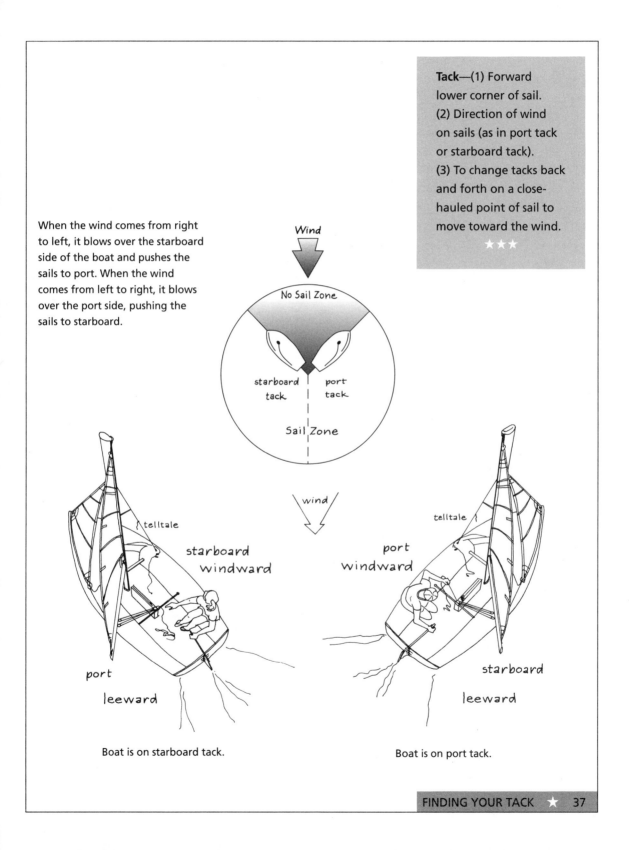

Wind

No Sail Zone

starboard tack | port tack

Sail Zone

wind

telltale

starboard windward

port windward

telltale

port leeward

starboard leeward

Boat is on starboard tack.

Boat is on port tack.

LEAVING
THE DOCK

With all your preparations complete, you are ready to leave the dock. It's helpful to have someone on shore who can untie the boat from the dock to cast you off. If you have to do it yourself, always return immediately to the tiller, the skipper's position, so you can take control of the boat before it has a chance to drift into other boats.

As the boat leaves the dock, you should be facing forward on the windward side of the boat. Naturally, the boom and mainsail will be on the opposite side of the boat from the wind, to leeward.

Remember, as you face forward you will feel the wind on one cheek. You should sit on that side so you can comfortably use your leeward hand for steering.

Facing forward, the skipper feels the wind on one cheek and uses the leeward hand (the one away from the wind) to hold the tiller.

STEERING AND SAIL TRIM

Now that you are leaving the dock, you need to learn how to steer your boat using a tiller and adjust your sails using the sheets.

The tiller is simply a handle; it controls the direction of the rudder under the stern. When you have the tiller in your hand, you are the skipper at the helm, and the adventure is yours to choose.

STEERING

When you turn the front wheel of a bicycle, the back wheel follows the front wheel inside the same track. A boat steers differently—from its back end, not its front. So when you push the tiller one way, you'll find that the bow turns in the *opposite* direction. If you want to steer to the left (to port), you push the tiller to the right, to starboard. To make the boat go to starboard, simply push the tiller to port.

This may seem confusing at first, but you'll be surprised how quickly you get used to it. Turning the direction you want to go will soon become natural and automatic, and is the beginning of your being in control as a skipper.

Notice that as you put the tiller in one direction, the stern swings out a little in the same direction, even though the bow is turning the way you want it to. The boat is pivoting around the front edge of the centerboard or keel, not around the rudder, as you might expect. So if you're close to a dock or another boat, remember that the stern swings out and that you must leave enough room to avoid bumping into it as you make your turn.

It takes forward motion to steer. This is because there must be a flow of water across the rudder for it to do its job. As the rudder moves, it changes the direction of the water flow. When that happens,

the boat changes course.

When you first leave the mooring or dock, it will take a moment to gain forward motion. You may even need a shove to get started. For that split second, you should keep the tiller in the center—until you're moving more forward than sideways—then begin to steer.

You'll find that to hold a steady course you have chosen, you need only make small motions of the tiller back and forth off the centerline. But you must make them often. Many factors combine to keep shifting your boat off course—wind, waves, current, fish.

By moving the tiller slightly, you can bring the boat back on course. This is called **correcting**. Pick a point on the horizon and steer toward it, correcting as you go. Or if you're out of sight of land, or in fog, correct frequently to the compass course you have chosen (refer to the sidebar on page 26 if you need to refresh your memory).

The only time you will have to make a big sweep of the tiller is when you are coming through a full turn, tacking or jibing. You'll learn about this in chapter 7.

So. You are in command. The wind is in your hair. Your boat is doing what you want it to. You are beginning to feel the magic of sailing.

A movement of the rudder forces the water moving over it to change direction, which in turn causes the boat to alter course.

pivot point

boat pivots around front of centerboard

centerboard

water flow

water hitting the rudder forces the stern to the side

tiller

rudder

Your boat may come with a tiller extension. If not, you can add one. It is an arm attached to the tiller by a little fitting that pivots all the way around. An extension is a handy device that helps you move around on board without letting go of the tiller.

tiller

tiller extension

universal joint

rudder

stern

TRIMMING
THE SAILS

To make the most of the wind, you must set your sails properly. This is called **trimming**. You know that the wind will come over one side of the boat and push the sails over to the other side. Once you have set your course, you will want to harness the power in your sails. You do this by easing out the mainsheet and jibsheet and then bringing them back to where they will work hardest for you. But how do you tell how far that is?

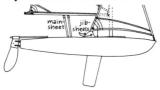

Here is a handy rule for both the mainsail and the jib: let the sail out until it begins to ripple along the front edge. (Remember, this is called luffing.) Once you have reached the luff point, pull the sheet in just enough for the luffing to stop. Then your sail is perfectly set.

Another good rule is: When in Doubt, Let it Out. Always think to yourself: "Is my sail out all the way to the luff point?" If not, let it out until you see luffing. Then pull in the sail until the luffing stops, but no farther. It is easy to pull in the sail too far by mistake. If you do, your boat will **stall.** Keep your sails on the verge of luffing.

Set your jib first. Then, to set your mainsail, face forward, with the mainsheet running along the top of the tiller, and hold both in your tiller hand. If you want to pull your mainsail in, do so with your free hand. If you want to let your mainsail out, continue to face forward; bring your free hand over to take the tiller, and with the other hand reach back to the cam cleat. Lift up the mainsheet to pull it out of the teeth of the cam cleat. It will ease itself out by sliding gradually through your hand.

When set correctly, the main and the jib will be lined up, or will lay, as sailors say, roughly parallel to each other.

Here are five hints to help you trim sail:

Hint 1: Luffing only happens along the forward edge of the sail. If you see movement in the middle, it could be that very light wind is moving the sail with the motion of the boat. If the sail is rippling along the leech edge, maybe you forgot to insert battens; tugging on the sheet won't help. For trimming, at least at this stage, you are only concerned with the forward edge.

Hint 2: As you get better at setting your sails, you will learn to anticipate the luff point and not actually need to see luffing. You will feel the proper set in your hands and arms, and the response of the boat. It is a sign of your growing skill and confidence.

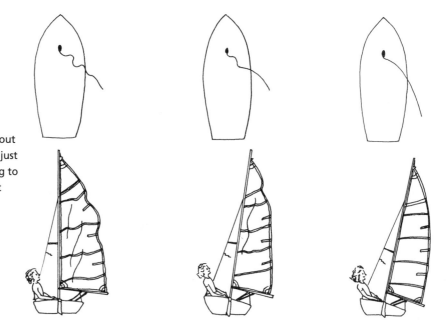

To set your sail, let it out until it luffs. Pull it in just enough for the luffing to stop. This keeps it just inside the luff point.

Let out the jib until it luffs, then pull it in until the luffing stops. Then it is set properly. Do the same for the mainsail. The two sails will naturally lay parallel to each other.

Stall—When a sail has lost its wind and no longer acts as an airfoil. You might stall a sail to slow down.

Trim—To adjust the sails to make the most of the wind.

★★★

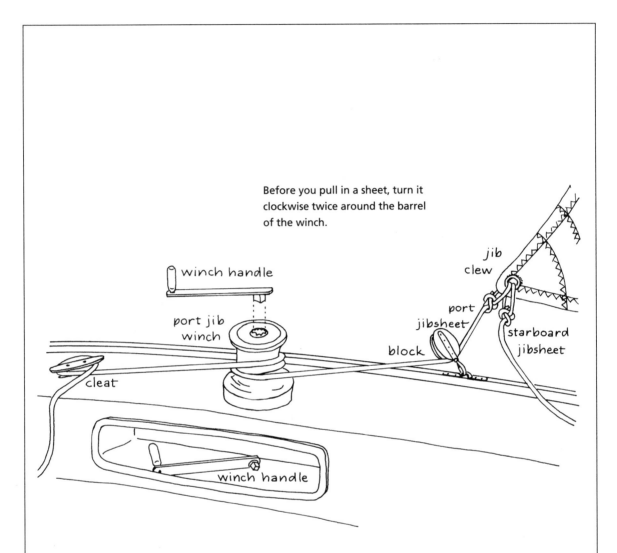

Before you pull in a sheet, turn it clockwise twice around the barrel of the winch.

winch handle

jib clew

port jib winch

port jibsheet

block

starboard jibsheet

cleat

winch handle

Hint 3: If your boat has a **winch** for the jibsheets, always be sure the sheet is wrapped twice around the winch in a clockwise direction before you pull on the line to tighten it.

Hint 4: Running a small sailboat alone takes some practice. You will need to be sure that you remain in control of the helm as you adjust the sheets. One trick is to steady the tiller between your knees and use your free hands to trim your sails to the luff point.

Hint 5: If you have a crew, each member should know that the skipper sets the course and the crew sets the jib. Sailing works better and is safer if everyone knows his or her job. The jib is set first. Then the skipper sets the mainsail.

HOW DOES WIND POWER YOUR SAILS?

Now that you know the basics of steering and sail handling, the next step in becoming a skilled sailor is learning more about how the wind powers your sails.

In this chapter, you will discover how a sail's shape makes the best use of the wind, and why a boat can sail at any angle to the wind, except in the no-sail zone.

You already know that wind blows on the sails to push the boat. The ancient Greek and Viking vessels, for example, could sail only with the wind pushing from behind, called **running.** Even the famous square-rigged clipper ships mostly sailed "before the wind," and could not sail as close to the wind as you can in your dinghy.

You can easily see how a boat is pushed forward when the wind is behind it. But how does the wind make your boat go forward when it blows on the sails from the side or even

from toward the bow?

Look more closely at the shape of your mainsail. When the wind is blowing, the sail is no longer a flat triangle. It is curved and flexible, with a deep pocket along the forward, or luff, edge. The curve is similar to the shape of this page when you push it up from the outside edge toward the center of the book and look from the top. To make it clear, imagine wind as being made up of pairs of particles. As the wind particles hit the leading edge of the sail, the luff, they separate and travel along both the inside and outside surfaces. The separated pairs race to reunite at the aft, or leech, edge.

But the wind particles on the outer curve of the sail have farther to travel around the hump of the curve than those on the inside curve. So the outside flow has to travel faster to catch up with the flow on the inside.

During this race, the wind on

the outside curve is spread out, so its pressure is lower. The wind on the inside piles up, and its pressure is higher.

The result is that the high pressure inside pushes on the inside of the sail, while the low pressure outside creates suction.

Together they make a push-pull effect, called an **airfoil** (see the drawing on page 48), that drives the boat forward even when it is sailing at an angle to the wind. Airplane wings are airfoils, too; a plane goes up and a sailboat goes forward in much the same way. Air rushing over the curved surfaces of wings lifts an airplane upward, just as wind over the curved surfaces of sails moves a boat forward.

While this push-pull action propels your boat forward and sideways, the centerboard prevents it from slipping sideways too much.

You can prove to yourself that this really works. Take a piece of notebook paper and hold it up horizontally by two corners in front of your face. The far edge of the paper will droop down because of gravity. Now blow hard along the *top* surface. The paper will be sucked back up to the horizontal. The faster-moving air on the top side creates lower pressure and the air underneath is slower and higher in pressure, causing an airfoil effect. Your sail, though it is vertical, not horizontal, works the same way.

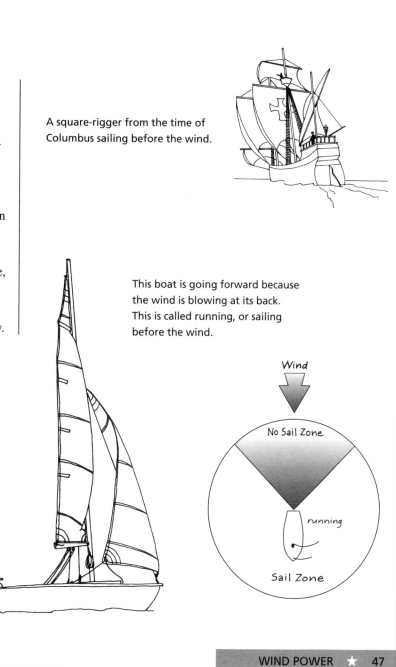

A square-rigger from the time of Columbus sailing before the wind.

This boat is going forward because the wind is blowing at its back. This is called running, or sailing before the wind.

WIND

Wind

No Sail Zone

running

Sail Zone

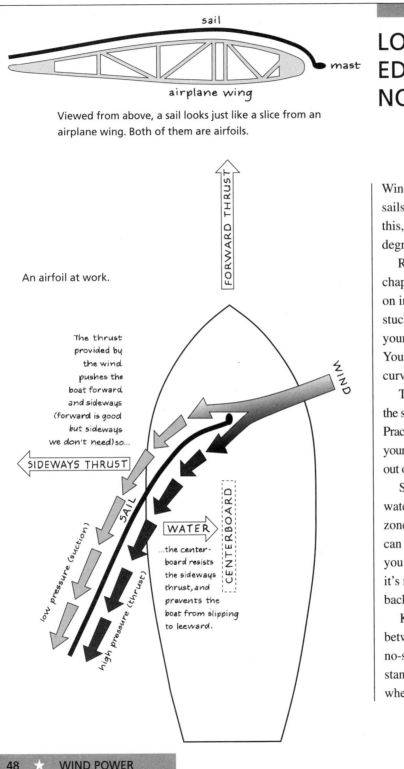

sail

mast

airplane wing

Viewed from above, a sail looks just like a slice from an airplane wing. Both of them are airfoils.

FORWARD THRUST

An airfoil at work.

The thrust provided by the wind pushes the boat forward and sideways (forward is good but sideways we don't need) so...

SIDEWAYS THRUST

WIND

SAIL

low pressure (suction)

high pressure (thrust)

WATER

...the centerboard resists the sideways thrust, and prevents the boat from slipping to leeward.

CENTERBOARD

LOCATING THE EDGE OF THE NO-SAIL ZONE

Wind needs to flow across your sails to create an airfoil. To do this, the sails must be at least 45 degrees away from the wind.

Remember the apple pie in chapter 3? Point the bow head on into the wind and you will be stuck in the no-sail zone with your sails luffing in the breeze. Your sails are unable to form a curve, or airfoil.

There is a distinct edge between the sail zone and the no-sail zone. Practice finding it. Gently move your boat across the edge, into and out of the two zones.

Sailors see every expanse of water in terms of these two zones. In the sail zone your boat can use the wind to go where you want to. In the no-sail zone, it's no-go. Except maybe backward.

Knowing the difference between the sail zone and the no-sail zone is vital to understanding sailing, especially when you need to react quickly.

SIX

POINTS OF SAIL,
Or "Where Am I in Relation to the Wind?"

Up to now, you've been steering a course and trimming your sails. Your world has been divided into two areas, one small, one large. You know now that you cannot sail in the small one—the no-sail zone. The large one, the remaining three-quarters of the apple pie, is the sail zone. In this chapter you'll learn about setting a course in the sail zone, and you'll discover how you can make your boat sail at different angles to the wind, called **points of sail**.

Points of sail are really not points at all, just names to describe the angle, or **heading**, of your boat in relation to the wind. The wind may be coming from your port side—port tack—or from your starboard side, if you're on starboard tack. Whichever side, sailors have developed names for a boat's angle to the wind. These names describe the whole range of sailing, from the very edge of the no-sail zone to running with the wind directly behind you.

Mastering the points of sail is the key to harnessing the wind's power to move your boat on a chosen course. Basically, the wind stays where it is. You change your point of sail by moving your bow closer to the wind or farther away from it.

When you have chosen a course, you know which tack you are on by which side of the boat the wind is coming from. But *where* off that side is it? Close to the bow? Near the stern?

To make the most of the wind, you must set your sails differently for each point of sail.

Heading—Direction your boat is going.

Point of Sail—Boat's position in relation to the wind.

★★★

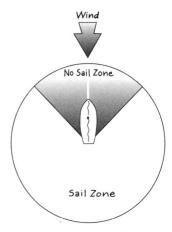

This is the pie with two slices missing to show the no-sail zone. The wind blows down the middle of the empty space, which extends for about 45 degrees on either side of center, 90 degrees altogether, or a quarter of the pie.

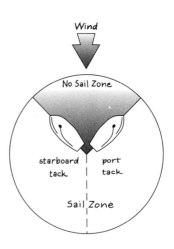

THE THREE MAIN POINTS OF SAIL

The first point of sail, when the wind is coming from just off your bow, is called **close hauled**. If your boat is as "close" to the wind (the no-sail zone) as it can be without being in the wind, its position is close hauled. Your sails must be "hauled" in tight to keep them from luffing.

If the wind is blowing directly over the side of your boat, **abeam**, or 90 degrees away from the bow, your point of sail is called a **beam reach**. Your sails will be at their luff point with the boom let out about halfway.

Abeam—At right angles to the side of the boat.
★★★

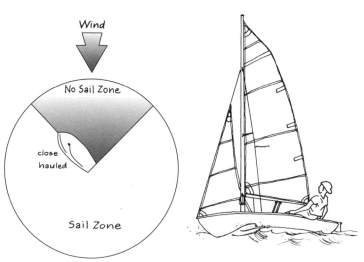

This boat is sailing as close to the wind as possible without spilling over into the no-sail zone. Its point of sail is close hauled. The sails are hauled in tight.

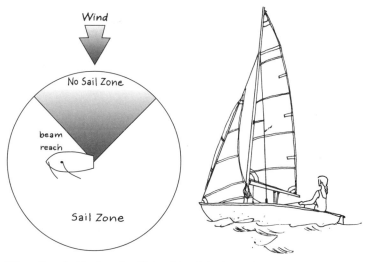

When the wind is directly off the side of the boat, the point of sail is called a beam reach. The sails are let out halfway.

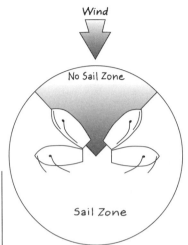

Two of these boats are on a starboard tack, one of them close hauled, the other on a beam reach. The other two boats are on a port tack. One is close hauled and the other is on a beam reach. Can you tell which is which?

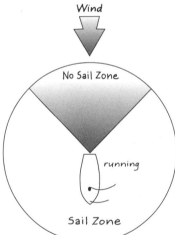

This boat is running with the wind. The wind is directly behind the stern, and the sail is at right angles to the wind. This boat is on a starboard tack because the wind has blown the mainsail over the port side.

In the previous illustrations, the boats are on a starboard tack—the wind is coming over the starboard side. But if the boats had been on the port tack, their points of sail would still be close hauled and beam reach. So now you can describe a boat's position by both the tack it is on and its point of sail.

A third point of sail is when the wind is coming from behind the boat, or from **astern**. As you learned in chapter 5, the boat is said to be running with the wind, or before the wind. We say "before" the wind because the boat is ahead of the wind with the wind pushing from behind.

When you're running before the wind, the sails are no longer acting as airfoils. All the power simply comes from the push of the wind on the back surfaces of the sails. The sails will find their luff point with the boom all the way out.

"Before the wind" was once the only way people knew how to sail. Paintings dating back to 3000 B.C. show that the Egyptians used large square sails on boats that could only travel when the wind came mostly over the stern. Columbus sailed the Atlantic from east to west with the tradewinds at his back. Then he waited for the seasonal wind change to blow him back to Europe.

The great square-rigged clipper ships could sail only a little closer to the wind than a beam reach. But today's fore-and-aft sails can sail with the wind from behind, the side, or ahead. Modern triangular sails, called Marconi, or jibheaded, can sail close hauled with the bow pointing very close to the wind.

Learn these first three points of sail by asking yourself two questions: "Where am I headed in relation to the wind? What point of sail am I on?" Soon you will start getting the answers right every time. Try looking at

MORE POINTS OF SAIL

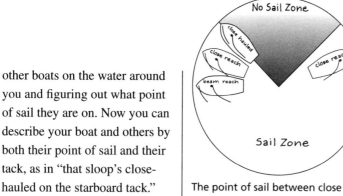

other boats on the water around you and figuring out what point of sail they are on. Now you can describe your boat and others by both their point of sail and their tack, as in "that sloop's close-hauled on the starboard tack."

On the ocean, the wind usually comes from the same direction for most of the day. On smaller bodies of water, the wind is more changeable or gusty. Any shifts in wind direction quickly become obvious, however, unless the wind is very light. Practice spotting exactly where your winds are coming from.

One way to keep track of wind direction while you are making a series of turns is to watch any landmarks that are close to the source of the wind, such as a line of trees or a water tower.

The point of sail between close hauled and beam reach is called a close reach. Here two boats are sailing on a close reach, one on a starboard tack, the other on a port tack. The sails are let out more than for close hauled, but not as much as for a beam reach.

There are two more points of sail, which cover the angles between the three main points of sail already described.

The fourth one lies between close hauled and beam reach. It is called a **close reach**.

The fifth one lies between beam reach and running. This is called a **broad reach**.

If you are on a close reach, your boom and sails should be set about halfway between being pulled in tight for close hauled and let out halfway for a beam reach.

If you are on a broad reach, your boom and sails should be eased, or let out, farther than the halfway point for a beam reach, but not all the way as for running.

The point of sail between a beam reach and running is called a broad reach. Here two boats are sailing on a broad reach, one on a starboard tack, the other on a port tack. The sails are let out more than for a beam reach, but not as much as for running.

TRIMMING AND THE POINTS OF SAIL

Learning the points of sail may feel like memorizing more new terms. Well, it is, in part. But learning these new words opens up your understanding of your boat's relationship to the wind. By knowing these terms you automatically imagine where you are on the wind, and this puts together the picture of the world with your boat in it. You pick the place to go, and the point of sail is a description of the angle you take on the wind to get there.

Here is a summary of the points of sail:

- When the boat is sailing close hauled, it will be as close to the wind as possible. The sails will be pulled in tight to stay just inside the luff point. They will be close to the centerline of the boat.
- As you move your bow farther away, or fall off, toward a close reach, then a beam reach, you can ease

your sails out as much as 45 degrees before reaching the luff point. Here the crew is responsible for easing and trimming sail to support the course being steered. As you continue to fall off from a beam reach to broad reach to run, you will need to ease out the mainsail as far as it can go before luffing.

So, as the boat falls off, or turns away from the wind, ease your sails bit by bit until you see a hint of luffing, then trim a bit to set them perfectly. Remember: When in Doubt, Let it Out.

If, when close hauled, you head up into the wind and slip into the no-sail zone, the boat will stop. Your sails will flap. This is called being **in irons**. To get out of irons, pull in the jib, and the wind will pull your bow to one side or another. Use the tiller to steer the bow toward the direction the jib is pulling you.

When you're close hauled,

sometimes the sails will begin to luff, but you are not in irons. Perhaps there has been a wind shift, or you have wandered across the edge of the no-sail zone. Trimming the sails can't stop the luffing because the sails are pulled all the way in. Instead, the helmsman must fall off a little—turn a little farther from the wind—so the sails can regain their pulling power. Sailing close hauled is different from the other points of sail because the sails stay pulled in tight. The helmsman adjusts the course by heading up or bearing off. If the sails luff, fall off. If the wind shifts, you might have to point up closer to it, staying as close to the wind as possible.

In Irons—When the bow is in the no-sail zone, the sails are luffing, and the boat isn't moving forward.

★★★

WHAT DOES A TELLTALE TELL?

Telltales, the strands of yarn tied to your shrouds, are extremely helpful. They flutter in the wind and show you instantly and clearly what direction the wind is coming from. Experienced sailors watch them constantly.

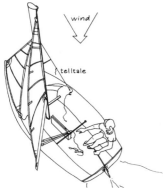

When the telltale is pointing to the middle of the mainsail, you are close hauled.

When the telltale is pointing directly toward the mast, you are on a beam reach.

When the telltale is pointing toward the forestay or bow, the wind is behind you pushing forward and you are running.

Make sure the sails are confirming what the telltale tells you.

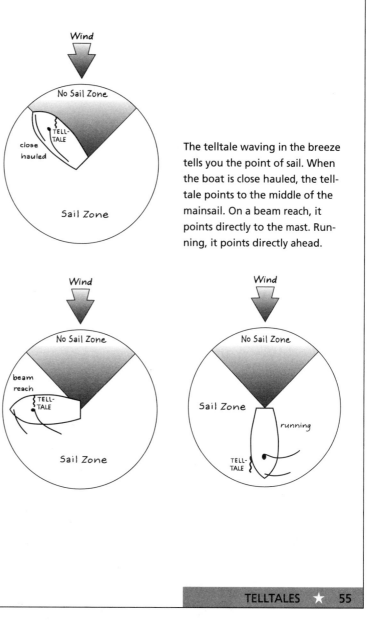

The telltale waving in the breeze tells you the point of sail. When the boat is close hauled, the telltale points to the middle of the mainsail. On a beam reach, it points directly to the mast. Running, it points directly ahead.

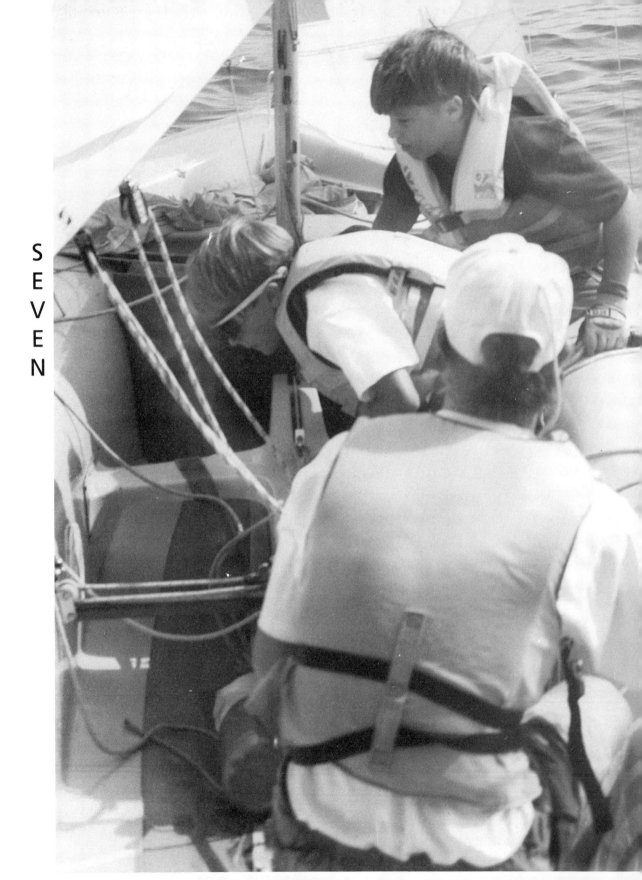

TURNING AROUND

Every vessel under sail is on either a starboard tack or a port tack. There are two ways to change from one to the other: by putting your bow through the no-sail zone, **coming about**, or by passing your stern through the no-sail zone, **jibing**. That is how a sailboat turns around.

COMING ABOUT

A sailboat can change tacks both upwind, with its bow briefly crossing through the no-sail zone, and downwind, which we'll talk about later. Turning your bow through the wind is called coming about.

When you push the tiller toward the boom, the bow will move into the wind and you will quickly lose speed, or **way**. Watch your sails during this move: they'll shift toward the center of the boat. When you get all the way into the no-sail zone, your sails will flap. Don't linger there. Go all the way

through the wind.

Keep your tiller pushed toward the mainsail when you are in the no-sail zone, and you will turn all the way through it and come out into the sail zone on the other side.

Your boom and sails will move across the centerline of the boat. As your boat changes direction, the sails pick up the wind on the new leeward side and pull you right out of the no-sail zone.

You will need to come at least 45 degrees past the source of the wind to get completely out of the no-sail zone. Then straighten the tiller—bring the helm **amidships**—to stop the turn and hold your new course.

You've just changed tacks. You used the momentum or speed you gained in sailing a straight course to cross through the no-sail zone and pick up the wind on the other side.

Let's look at what happens. When the boat begins to turn,

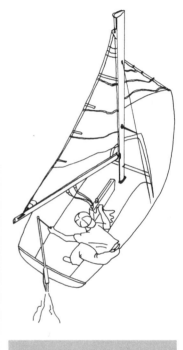

This boat is coming about, turning around from a port to a starboard tack. You push the tiller to leeward, and the bow moves through the no-sail zone. The jib and mainsail move across the boat and are set on the new leeward side.

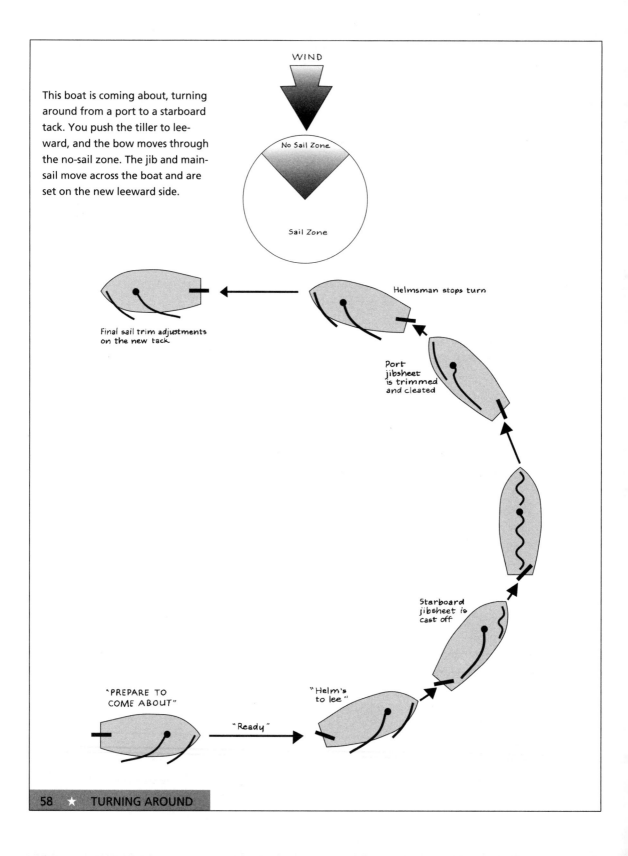

WIND

No Sail Zone

Sail Zone

Helmsman stops turn

Final sail trim adjustments on the new tack

Port jibsheet is trimmed and cleated

Starboard jibsheet is cast off

"PREPARE TO COME ABOUT"

"Ready"

"Helm's to lee"

leeward   WIND   windward

your mainsail and jib will start to luff. As the jib luffs, let go of the jibsheet on the leeward side. The jib will flap its way through the no-sail zone and move to the other side of the boat. As you steady the tiller on your new course, trim, or pull in, the jibsheet so that the jib is just inside its luff point. You may need to pull very hard to trim the jibsheet. If there is a lot of wind, you can ease the strain by "luffing up" briefly—just long enough to tighten the jibsheet. To tighten the new leeward jibsheet on boats equipped with a winch, take two wraps around the winch and pull. Then cleat it: once around the jam cleat is all it takes.

The boom and the mainsail will also move across the boat from the old leeward side to the new leeward side. Duck out of the way of the boom, if necessary, so it doesn't hit your head. You or one of your crew should let out the mainsail, so

the sail can move across, and then pull it tight just inside the new luff point.

Having changed tack, you must move your body to the new windward side. Remember, as skipper you should always face forward to see where your boat is headed. (As you change sides, pass the tiller from hand to hand behind your back.) It takes hand and eye coordination—and practice—to change your whole body position and still steer a straight course.

Settle yourself on the new windward side. Your boat will take a moment to regain the momentum you had on the previous tack. Be patient and do not oversteer.

Preparations for coming about are very important. If you have a crew, you need to warn them that you intend to change tacks by saying: "Prepare to come about" or "Ready about."

This tells them to pay attention. The crew should respond quickly by saying: "Ready," as soon as they are ready. (Even if you are sailing singlehanded, or on your own, you can say "Prepare to come about" to yourself just to get in the ready mode.)

Next you call to the crew (or tell yourself): "Helm's to lee," or "Hard alee." This means you are pushing the tiller to the leeward side.

COMING ABOUT IN FOUR MOVEMENTS

For help in coming about, remember these four simple movements:
• Movement of jib from one side to the other.
• Movement of body from one side of the boat to the other.
• Movement of mainsheet from one hand to the other.
• Movement of tiller from one hand to the other.

JIBING

When you change tack with the bow passing through the no-sail zone, you are coming about. The second way to change from one tack to another is jibing. It is the opposite of coming about. The stern, instead of the bow, passes through the no-sail zone.

Preparation for jibing is slightly different from that for coming about. But it starts in a similar way. Tell your crew: "Prepare to jibe!"

In coming about, your mainsail and jib were already pulled in tight and simply luffed themselves into the center of the boat as the bow turned into the wind. Then they luffed over to the new leeward side.

In jibing, your bow will be turning away from the wind. That means you will be going from a beam or broad reach, or even running, on one tack to the same thing on the other tack. Therefore, your boom and mainsail will be set all the way out. As you move your stern across the wind, the change of tack downwind brings the boom swinging hard across the cockpit without ever luffing. Duck, so you aren't in the path of the boom as it crosses. The boom may have been named by a sailor who wasn't careful.

To stop any wild swinging of the boom, you must first center it by pulling all the way in on the mainsheet. Center the boom when you shout, "Prepare to jibe!"

Your crew responds, "Ready." That means they are ready to cast off the jibsheet on the old leeward side and pull it in on the new leeward side as the boat turns and picks up the wind again.

When everyone is ready, and you have sheeted the boom in to the middle of the boat, give the command to jibe, "Jibe ho!" (This may make you feel like a character in a Hollywood pirate movie, but it will have to do until someone comes up with a better expression.)

On the command "Jibe ho," pull the tiller to the windward side, meaning toward you.

This sends the stern through the no-sail zone and moves the bow away from the wind. The jib should move quickly to the new leeward side and fill. In contrast to coming about, you will not have to use any real force to pull in the jib on the new side. It will move over easily and wait for you or your crew to adjust it.

As the mainsail jibes over, ease the boom out, again to its desired reach or run position. As with coming about, you will have to move your body to the new windward side, still facing forward, and changing the tiller and mainsheet from one hand to the other behind your back.

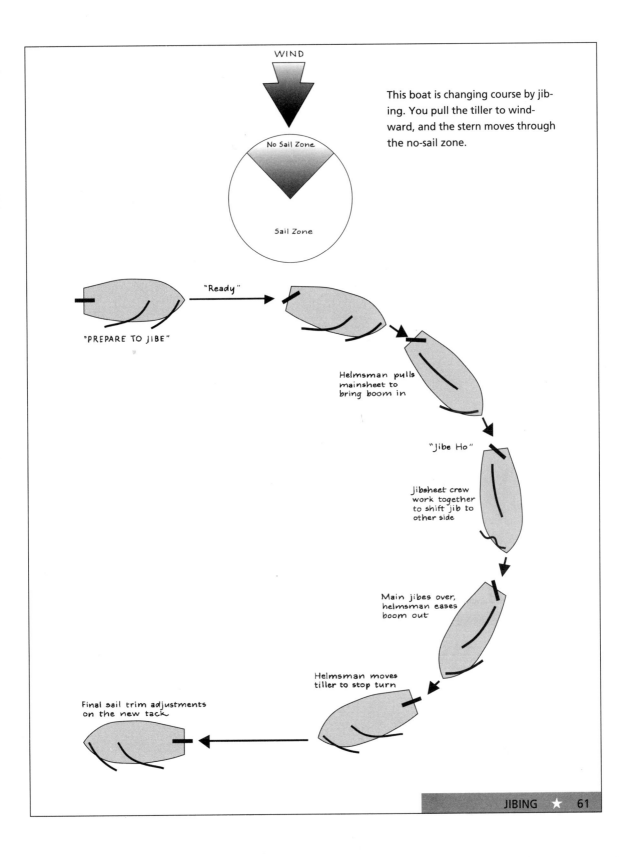

WIND

No Sail Zone

Sail Zone

This boat is changing course by jibing. You pull the tiller to windward, and the stern moves through the no-sail zone.

"Ready"

"PREPARE TO JIBE"

Helmsman pulls
mainsheet to
bring boom in

"Jibe Ho"

Jibsheet crew
work together
to shift jib to
other side

Main jibes over,
helmsman eases
boom out

Helmsman moves
tiller to stop turn

Final sail trim adjustments
on the new tack

TACKING UPWIND, JIBING DOWNWIND

You now know how coming about or jibing enables you to turn around by moving from one tack to another. This knowledge allows you to navigate to a destination in the no-sail zone. And, more important, it means you can now sail anywhere, regardless of the direction of the wind.

Let's say a dock with a sandwich shop is directly into the wind and you're hungry. You know you can't sail upwind in a straight line. Until now, you could only sail near to the dock, missing it by about 45 degrees, on whichever tack you chose. But knowing how to change tacks means you can take a zigzag course of small come-abouts. This is called **beating to windward** or tacking upwind. Eventually you will work your way to the dock by **tacking,** that is, changing from one tack to the other. On each tack you will be close hauled so that you sail as close to the wind and as close to

a direct course toward your destination as possible.

Just as coming about allows you to tack on an upwind course, jibing enables you to tack on a downwind course. Upwind you will be close hauled. Downwind you will be on a broad reach or running.

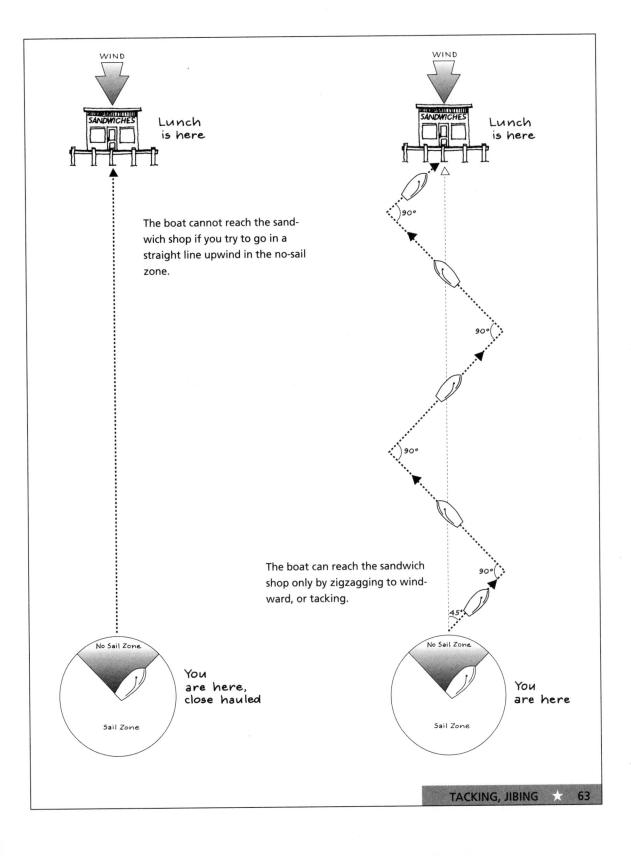

WIND

SANDWICHES

Lunch
is here

The boat cannot reach the sandwich shop if you try to go in a
straight line upwind in the no-sail
zone.

The boat can reach the sandwich
shop only by zigzagging to windward, or tacking.

No Sail Zone

Sail Zone

You
are here,
close hauled

WIND

SANDWICHES

Lunch
is here

90°

90°

90°

90°

45°

No Sail Zone

Sail Zone

You
are here

HOW NOT TO GO FULL CIRCLE AND OTHER HINTS

Practice is the key to successful tacking. You have to learn to move the tiller smoothly and decisively, but not *too* quickly. You must also judge the point in your turn where you need to correct, or bring the tiller back amidships. If you hold the tiller hard over for too long, the boat will keep going in a circle. To prevent that, anticipate by straightening the tiller slightly before you reach your new tack.

Many beginners forget which way to push the tiller at the start of a turn. Here are two sentences to remind you:

Coming about is tiller TOWARD the sails and the bow TOWARD the wind.

Jibing is tiller AWAY from the sails and the bow off, or AWAY from, the wind.

It is important to have enough wind and forward motion when you start to come about. That way you can complete the passage of the bow through the no-sail zone without stalling.

Remember to center the boom as you jibe by pulling in the mainsheet as you turn. Continue to hold course and look forward.

In previous chapters, we talked about the no-sail zone as a place to stop and raise your sails. But in coming about *and* jibing, you'll find that you can use the no-sail zone as a passage for changing tacks.

If you go back to the pie circle in the illustrations, you will find you can sail all the way around it without stopping anywhere. Being in the no-sail zone no longer means being unable to move.

When you know how to pass through the no-sail zone, you also will know how to set your sails for every tack and every point of sail.

Let's go through the full circle. The position of your sails tells you where you are. Coming out of the no-sail zone, close hauled, your sails are close to

the center of the boat. They will move away from the center as you move your bow away from the wind until you are all the way downwind, ready to jibe. After jibing, the sails gradually will ease all the way out. You work them in again as your bow moves closer to the wind, to close reach, close hauled, and then you return to the no-sail zone.

Now you can identify your tack and point of sail for every position of the wind on the boat. You know how to catch the wind and how to harness its energy. Now for that sandwich!

Now you can see the tack and point of sail you are on for every position of the wind.

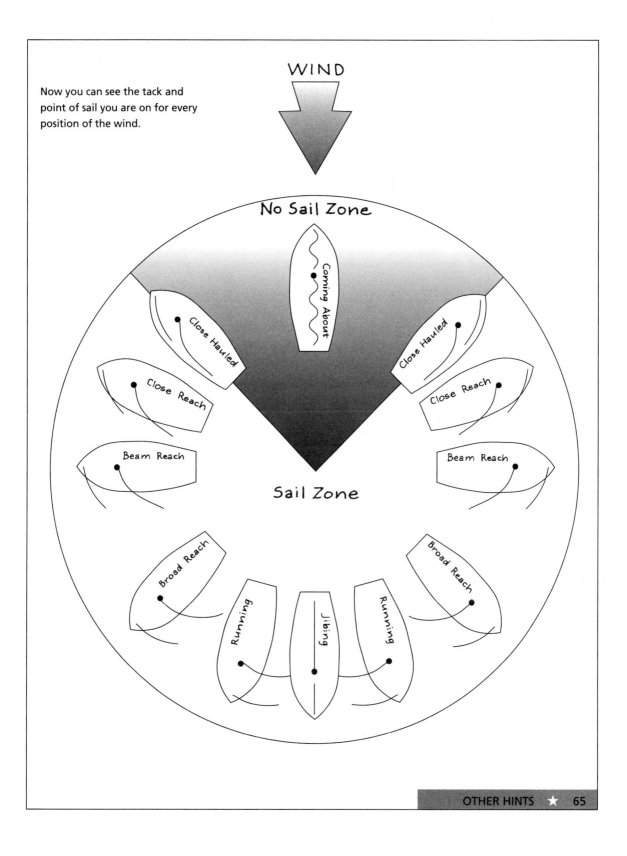

WIND

No Sail Zone

Coming About

Close Hauled

Close Hauled

Close Reach

Close Reach

Beam Reach

Beam Reach

Sail Zone

Broad Reach

Broad Reach

Running

Jibing

Running

HEELING

As the wind picks up speed, your boat is likely to **heel**. In fact, its hull is designed to sail fastest under a certain amount of heel, no more than 15 degrees. Though your boat will lean over with the weight of the wind in its sails, you and your crew can keep it from heeling too far by shifting your weight. Tuck your toes under a **thwart** or, with some boats, a **hiking strap** that runs along the sides of the centerboard. Sit way out over the windward side. Hold on to the mainsheet or jibsheet and lean back to try to hold the boat flat. This balancing is called **hiking**. Expect at least one part of you to get wet while you're hiking.

Heeling is a blast on a breezy day, maybe during a tight race against friends. Your boat is built to lean quite a bit without swamping or tipping over, so enjoy the feeling.

Successful heeling is a matter of precisely balancing your body weight against the amount of wind in your sails at any given moment. If the wind changes and you feel you are heeling too far, ease the main out to spill some wind. Unsuccessful heeling, of course, means capsizing, which we'll cover in the next chapter.

Heel—Leaning of the boat to one side in response to the wind.

Hike—To balance heeling boat with body weight.

Thwart—Seat that extends across the cockpit.

★★★

hiking strap

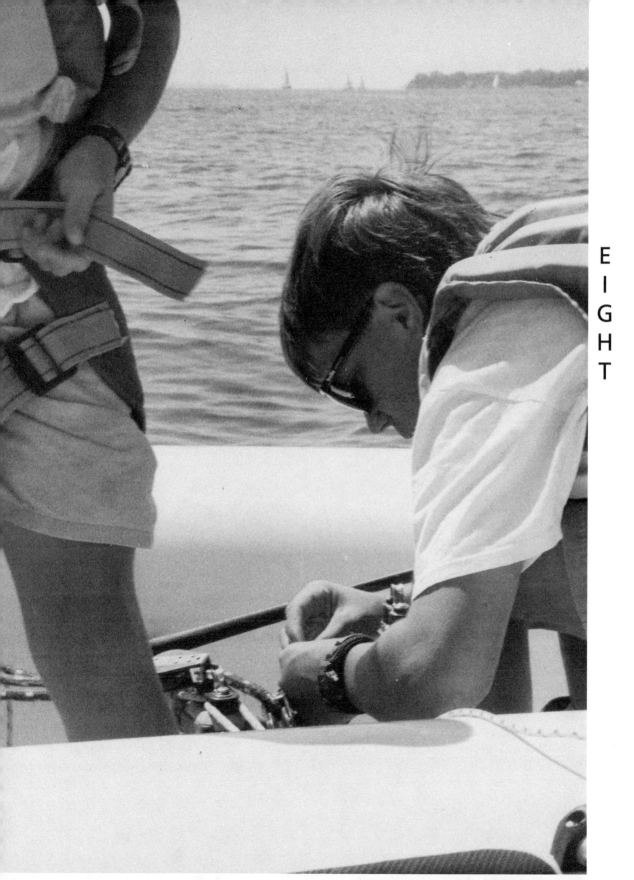

EMERGENCIES

As your skills and confidence build, sailing becomes more fun. With the freedom and control to turn your bow upwind or downwind, you can head for a swimming beach, a great fishing spot, a deserted island.

But things can go wrong. In chapter 2, we discussed the importance of being prepared. In this chapter we look at three possible emergencies—capsizing, crew overboard, and getting caught in a thunderstorm.

With forethought, common sense, and quick action, none of these situations need be more than a challenge to your seamanship. Always remember, though, that Nature doesn't play favorites. In dealing with an actual emergency, it helps enormously if you have practiced what you will do when trouble shows up.

Wear your life jacket. You don't want to have to worry about finding it and putting it on when an emergency happens. If you're wearing it, it will keep you afloat even if a jibing boom suddenly bonks you in the head and pitches you into the water.

CAPSIZING

Keeled boats generally will not tip over, or capsize, but boats with centerboards and daggerboards can and sometimes do. Most small boats are designed to turn upright without too much difficulty after capsizing. Capsizing isn't scary or dangerous on a pleasant day if you know how to swim.

But there should be no "if." Learn to swim, *then* learn to sail.

Capsizing usually results from heeling too far or an accidental jibe. If you feel in real danger of tipping over, luff the mainsail at once, by letting the mainsheet fly. If your boat does go over on its side, stay with it; never swim away. You must do several things quickly. First, make sure that no one is trapped under the boat or tangled in the rigging. If they are, help them to get free.

Next, stand on the center-

Use your body weight on the centerboard and pull on the shrouds and gunwale to right a capsized boat.

centerboard

shroud

gunwale

board as quickly as possible to prevent the boat from turning completely upside down. Be sure the mainsheet is free, and free the jibsheets so the sails will not fill with water when the boat is capsized or with air when it is rightside up again. If possible, try to swim the bow around into the no-sail zone.

Then swim back to the side of the boat, grab the gunwale or the shrouds, stand on the centerboard, and lean back with all your weight. This leverage should slowly bring the boat back up. Hang on. Pull and

slither yourself aboard over the side or the stern. Things will be a jumble. Start to bail, unless you have a self-bailing cockpit and can "sail it dry." Get one sail sheeted in and pulling enough to get some way on, and then steer a forgiving course, like a beam reach, to give yourself and your crew a few moments to sort yourselves out.

If your boat turns upside down, you should still use the centerboard for leverage, but it will need much more effort. Even if the centerboard has slipped back down into the hull, it is possible to bring one jibsheet up over the hull, stand on the opposite gunwale, and gradually haul the mast back to the surface and then upright, though this is a real feat of strength.

Above all, remember: *Stay with your boat.* It floats, it doesn't get tired, and it is visible a long way off. Don't even *think* of swimming ashore.

"CREW OVERBOARD!"

The shout of "Crew overboard" means someone has accidentally fallen or been knocked into the water. It happens without warning and can be frightening. It is essential that you do not panic.

If the person is not wearing a life jacket, toss one—or your throwable cushion—*at once,* both for flotation and to mark the spot.

Then, carefully keeping an eye on the person in the water, quickly jibe around. If you are close to the wind, it may be faster to come about rather than jibing. Circle to leeward of the person in the water so that when you get there you can head the bow into the wind, and luff the sails so you slow to a stop. You want to stop right next to the person in the water to make the rescue. Be careful not to swamp the boat by having all the weight on one side as you pull the person on board. Practice this maneuver using a buoyant seat cushion in place of a person overboard. Practice until you can rescue the cushion both by jibing and coming about, and from various points of sail. You may save a life someday.

When a person falls overboard, immediately throw out a life jacket or life ring. Besides providing buoyancy, it is a visual marker.

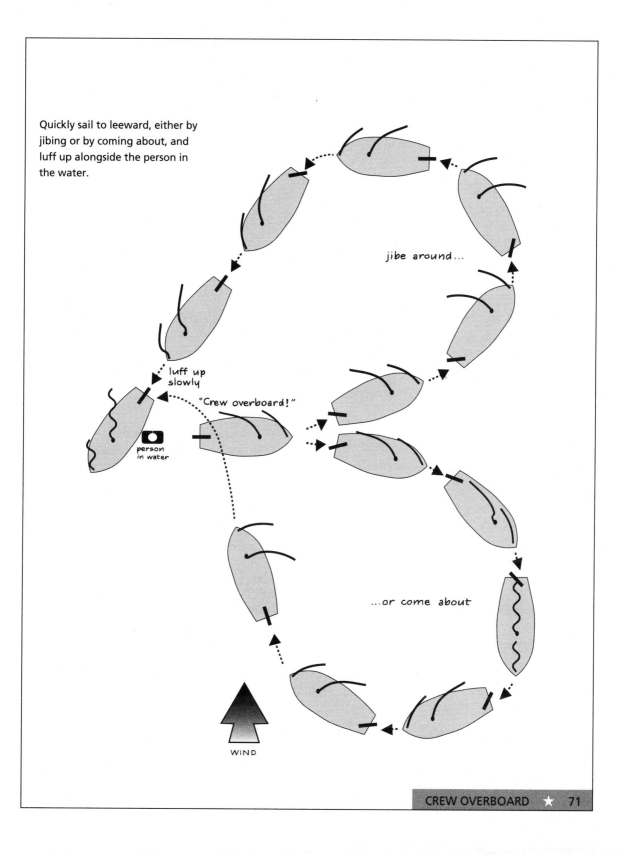

Quickly sail to leeward, either by
jibing or by coming about, and
luff up alongside the person in
the water.

jibe around...

luff up
slowly

"Crew overboard!"

person
in water

...or come about

WIND

THUNDER-STORMS

If bad weather is predicted, do not go sailing. Skippers should choose not to be on the water in a storm. If a squall does blow up suddenly while you are sailing, you and your crew should have your life jackets strapped on securely. Reduce sail area and head toward a safe harbor.

Good sailors are always careful about weather. As the old rhyme says:

"Red sky at night, sailor's delight;

"Red sky in the morning, sailors take warning."

A red sunset usually means clear, dry air. A red dawn can mean rain. Such observations are useful, but check local weather forecasts before setting out on any sail longer than a quick tootle around the harbor. Radio and television carry forecasts, and most cable television systems have a 24-hour weather channel that gives wind and wave conditions for boaters. Check your barometer:

when it falls rapidly, wet weather or a storm is coming; a rising barometer indicates fair or clearing weather. You can also call the weather number in the front of the phone book.

Be alert for *small craft advisories*. These warnings mean that there could be winds up to 20 knots, plus 3-foot-high waves. Such conditions are hazardous for boats under 24 feet.

Stay at home with a good book if you hear *special marine warnings,* when winds of 34 knots are expected; *gale warnings,* with prolonged winds up to 45 knots; *storm warnings,* with up to 65 knots of wind; or *hurricane warnings,* with winds of 65-plus knots.

When you hear these warnings, batten down your boat by doubling up any tiedown or mooring lines and stowing any loose gear.

Big storm fronts are usually forecast 12 to 48 hours ahead.

Small, isolated thunderstorms are much less predictable, a local hazard that regional weather forecasts often can't pinpoint.

Thunderstorms can show up quickly, with high winds and lots of lightning. Typically, they appear on hot, humid, and hazy summer days. Everything feels still on the water, but you will see towering, puffy clouds, gray in color. These are cumulonimbus clouds, better known as thunderheads. They are formed by warm, moist air rising to meet cooler air above.

If you are on the water, at the first sign of these gathering storm clouds, put on your life jacket and head in. It will be much more difficult to reach safety if you wait until the windless calm that occurs before a storm. When the storm does hit, it will bring cold, fierce winds from a new direction.

If you have not made it in by then, you have three choices:

Cumulonimbus clouds, known as thunderheads, form when warm, moist air rises to meet cold air. Big and puffy, the clouds grow darker as the storm approaches. The higher the top of the upper cloud mass, known as the anvil, the more ferocious the storm when it reaches you.

- Reduce sail area and continue racing for home port.
- Reduce sail area and make for a nearer safe haven where you can anchor or tie up to a mooring.
- Ride out the storm as best you can, either under **bare poles** or **hove to** (see illustration on page 74).

Bare Poles—Sailing without sails set, generally in a heavy wind.

★★★

REDUCING SAIL AREA

When storm winds blow, you have to decide early on what to do with your sails. It is best to be overly cautious. We recommend taking down one sail.

If the wind is behind you, take down your mainsail and leave your jib up. That will give you enough sail to keep moving into port at a safe but not reckless speed. If the wind is close to the bow, take down the jib. You can still move upwind using the mainsail. Do not cleat the mainsheet. Keep it in your hand so that you can luff and spill air quickly if wind threatens to knock you over.

Many small boats can be **roller-reefed**. Pull your boom off the gooseneck fitting until it turns. Then, while lowering the halyard, turn the boom so the sail wraps around it. Start by reducing your sail area by a third.

To hold your position in a storm, you can heave to. Let your mainsail all the way out so it luffs, pull your jib in on the windward side across the mast, and tie the tiller loosely so it's immobilized on the leeward side. The boat will move very slowly, if at all. You shouldn't need to steer, but don't leave your helm, just in case.

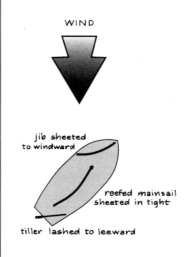

WIND

jib sheeted
to windward

reefed mainsail
sheeted in tight

tiller lashed to leeward

Heaving to.

ANCHORING DURING A STORM

If you reach a protected bay, or some other safe haven, you can anchor during a storm. Follow these steps:

• Tie the free end of your anchor rode (the line attached to your anchor) to the mast. Make sure the rest of the line is neatly coiled and not tangled so it can run smoothly when you let the anchor go.
• Turn the boat into the wind and luff the sails.
• Drop the anchor gently off the bow and let the anchor rode follow smoothly after it, until you feel no more anchor weight. Then pay out line as your boat drifts backward with the wind, until you have out about 10 feet of anchor rode for every foot of water depth. You will probably use all the anchor rode you have.
• Tug hard on the anchor several

A multipurpose Danforth anchor. The boat pulling on the anchor rode makes the sharp points of the anchor dig more firmly into the bottom.

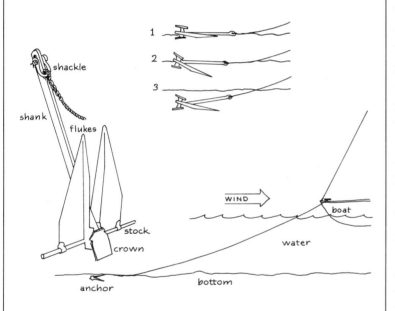

RIDING OUT A STORM

The wind may become so strong that your boat starts to heel over beyond your control, even with reduced sail area or when hove to. If this happens, and you can't reach shelter, you must ride out the storm under bare poles.

This is the least desirable option. Your aim must be to keep the boat moving as slowly as possible while the storm blows by, which usually takes 20 minutes to an hour.

Head into the wind, make certain your centerboard is all the way down, and take down both sails. Secure the mainsail by wrapping it up in itself, and use the mainsheet to lash it to the boom. Stuff the jib in the bow and wrap the jibsheets around it to keep it from catching air.

times to make certain it has caught on the bottom, and cleat the line on your bow cleat.
- Lower the sails and tie them down with their sheets so they do not billow in the wind.
- Stay low in the boat and wait out the storm. Watch for other vessels that may be able to offer help.

- Take note of a landmark to help you judge if you are dragging your anchor and drifting.

The type of anchor you use depends on whether the bottom is rock, sand, mud, or seaweed. A good multipurpose anchor is a Danforth.

LIGHTNING

FOG

PRACTICE FOR THE UNEXPECTED

The chances of your boat being struck by lightning are exceedingly small.

The best protection from lightning is to head in to port before the storm. Failing that, you should stay low in the boat and keep your hands off wire shrouds, the mast (if metal), metal fittings.

Fog can roll in quickly and present you with three problems: there is no wind, you can't see, and you can't be seen. The best thing to do in fog is make noise. Use your whistle, or bang your paddle against the mast to let other boats know you are there. If you have a rough idea whether land is east or west, you could sail slowly toward land. Another option is to sail a compass course toward shore. See the sidebar on page 26 for more on using a compass.

You may sail for many happy days and never need any of the advice in this chapter. But the good skipper is always prepared for emergencies.

Practice the crew-overboard maneuver described earlier. Try capsizing and righting your boat in calm, shallow water close to shore. Be careful not to go all the way over in water too shallow for your mast. Practice anchoring. Practice heaving to in a gentle breeze. (It's a great way to take time out from sailing while you eat a picnic lunch.) Reduce your sail area to see how it might feel to ride out a storm. In each case, practice will give you confidence to cope with a real emergency—quickly and without panic.

COMING HOME
and Other Topics

There comes a time when every sailor yearns for home. After a day's adventure, it's time to come back to dry land and share your sea stories. As this chapter explains, getting home means figuring out how to approach a mooring, dock, or beach. After that, your boat needs to be de-rigged. Finally, you must decide what to put away and what to leave with the boat.

This chapter also includes other information you need about tides, current, and navigation rules for avoiding collisions.

SAILING TO A MOORING

Sailing to a mooring is very similar to getting to a person overboard. Sail to a point two boat lengths to leeward of the mooring—less if the wind is strong, or your boat is a very light one. Head up quickly into the no-sail zone and drift straight for the mooring. Drop your sails as you coast the two boat lengths to a stop at the mooring. Get the mooring line aboard quickly and loop it around the bow cleat before you do anything else.

If you are by yourself or overshoot your mark, you can let the mooring roll along the side of the boat. You have a second chance with your jam cleat. When you can, reach directly over the side to grab the pennant, the loop of braided line. Hang it quickly over your jam cleat. The cleat will take the strain. It will stop your boat if you still have momentum. When you're ready, walk the mooring line to the bow.

DOCKING

As you near the dock, check for other boats already tied up there, and check for wind direction. It may be blowing onshore, from somewhere behind you toward the dock; offshore, generally from the dock to you; or alongshore, sideways across the dock. You therefore need three different docking tactics, all of them based on what you already know by now.

Docking is not that different from picking up your mooring. You just have less room to do it. By now you know how to bring your boat to a stop—by heading up into the no-sail zone. A dock is a heavy, fixed object, so you should approach it in a cautious, calm, and unhurried way. When you get close, you may feel that you are going too fast or coming in at the wrong angle. Just turn around and start over. Even experienced sailors sometimes make several tries.

This skipper and crew positioned themselves to windward of the dock before approaching. Then they turned into the wind to bring down the mainsail.

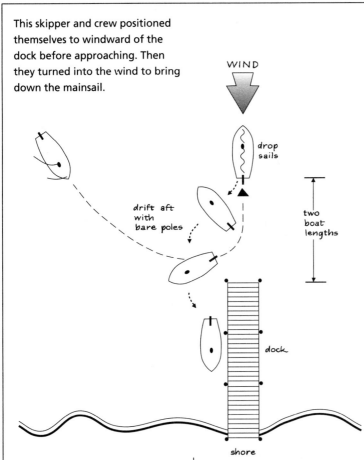

WIND

drop
sails

drift aft
with
bare poles

two
boat
lengths

dock

shore

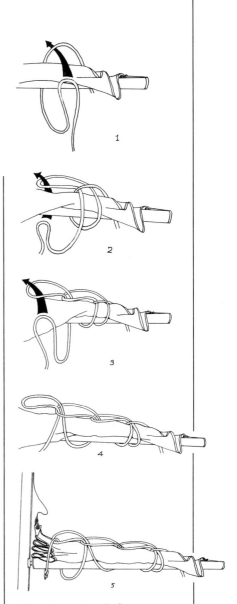

1

2

3

4

5

ONSHORE WIND

If the wind is behind or slightly off to one side and pushing you into the dock, you can just drop your sails and drift in. Head to a point to windward and within a couple of boat lengths of the dock. Turn into the no-sail zone. Your sails will luff. Release the sheets and drop both sails.

As soon as the mainsail is all the way down, quickly roll it up and lash it to the boom as your bow drifts toward the dock. Use the mainsheet to make a **timber hitch**—a series of loops around the boom that can come undone with one pull on the end of the sheet.

Even under bare poles, your boat will sail slightly. Stay with your tiller to guide her in. In a good wind you might be pushed in faster than you expect. With some way on, you can steer and turn broadside to the dock just as you reach it.

Roll up the mainsail after you lower it. Use the mainsheet to tie a timber hitch: Loop the sheet through itself and around the boom. The hitch comes undone with one pull on the end of the sheet.

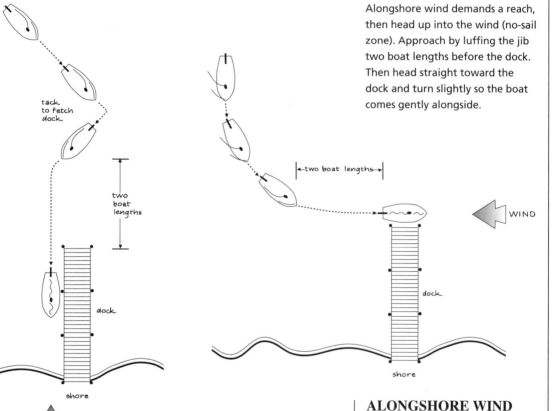

This boat is positioning itself by sailing parallel to the dock a boat length or so away. The skipper turns into the wind to head for the intended docking spot.

tack to fetch dock

two boat lengths

dock

shore

WIND

Alongshore wind demands a reach, then head up into the wind (no-sail zone). Approach by luffing the jib two boat lengths before the dock. Then head straight toward the dock and turn slightly so the boat comes gently alongside.

|←two boat lengths→|

WIND

dock

shore

OFFSHORE WIND

If the wind is in front, you have to sail to the dock on a close reach or close hauled. Keep both sails up. Visualize your angle of approach. Note the angle of the wind off the dock. Your goal is to sail parallel to the side of the dock a boat length or so away. When your mast is even with your docking spot, turn sharply into the wind, release your sheets, and put your nose on the dock right on the spot you picked.

ALONGSHORE WIND

If the wind is blowing roughly parallel to the shore, the best course is to come in on a close reach, then round up dead into the no-sail zone a length or so before the end of the dock. Your boat should stop, sails up but luffing, so you can step ashore and secure your bow line to a dock cleat.

TYING UP AND THE BOWLINE

The best knot to use when tying up is a **bowline**. It will hold tight without slipping but is very easy to undo. The bowline has plenty of other uses around the boat. If you break a shackle, it can hold your halyard to your sail, and it can secure the jibsheets to the jib. The bowline is a difficult knot at first, but worth mastering.

A simple way to remember how to make this very useful knot is to think of a rabbit running around a tree and back down its hole.

1. Make a loop in the line, the rabbit's hole.

2. Take the end of the line, the rabbit, and bring it out of the hole.

3. The rabbit runs behind the tree and back down the hole.

4. Pull the rabbit in one direction and the tree in the other.

5. The finished bowline. You've made a knot that will not slip, yet can be easily untied.

BEACHING YOUR BOAT

If you want to beach your boat for a picnic, simply approach, luff to look for a good spot, and slowly drift or sail gently ashore. Lift the centerboard gradually as the water gets shallow, and if your rudder is hinged, make sure it bumps up too. When you actually touch bottom, let the sheets fly, jump into the water with the bow line in hand, and haul your boat up onto the beach. Drop the sails. As insurance, even if there isn't much wind, take a couple of turns of the bow line around a tree or rock, or dig in your anchor somewhere nearby.

PADDLING

PUTTING YOUR BOAT TO BED

There will be a time when the wind dies and you are floating around with droopy sails. Don't despair. Turn to your other source of power—yourself. It is time to paddle. If you are alone, lift the rudder out of the water and sit on the stern. Dip the paddle blade fully into the water and pull it back. You can steer by changing sides every few strokes.

If you have a crew, you don't need to lift the rudder. Instead, have the crew drop the jib and paddle from the bow while you steer. Change jobs often. It's tedious work, but better than sitting motionless. Besides, the odds are that if other sailors with engines see you paddling, they may offer you a tow. And if they don't, you *will* get home eventually.

Most dinghies or small boats have no sail cover to protect them from the ultraviolet rays of the sun, which means sails should be put away after each use. On bigger boats that do have covers, the mainsail stays rolled up on the boom, secured every few feet with **sail stops** to prevent the wind from tearing it loose. The sail cover goes over the **furled** sail.

Removing the sails is easy. Simply reverse the steps you learned in chapter 1 to rig the boat, but with one caution: When you unhook your halyard, be careful not to let it fly loose or go up the mast. Clip it to anything handy, even temporarily to your belt, if necessary. Rescuing a wayward halyard is a pain in the neck you can do without. When you finally secure the shackle, pull tight on the other end of the halyard and cleat it to its mast cleat.

If you are packing your sails, first spread them flat on the

ground. Fold them back and forth like an accordion along the two long edges, the luff and the leech, pulling the head to the foot. It's easiest to do this with two people, one standing at the tack, the other at the clew, working as a team.

When you have folded the sail all the way to the head, roll it up like a sleeping bag, from the tack to the clew, so that the clew is ready for putting on first next time out.

The jib usually goes in a bag, along with its sheets. An experienced sailor bags the jib so that the tack corner goes in last, so it comes out first.

We recommend covering your boat with a piece of canvas or tarpaulin known as a **boom tent.** It drapes snugly over the boom and is tied down over the gunwales. Or it can be secured to the boat's cradle or trailer for longer-term storage. A boom tent is especially important in winter, but also protects the boat

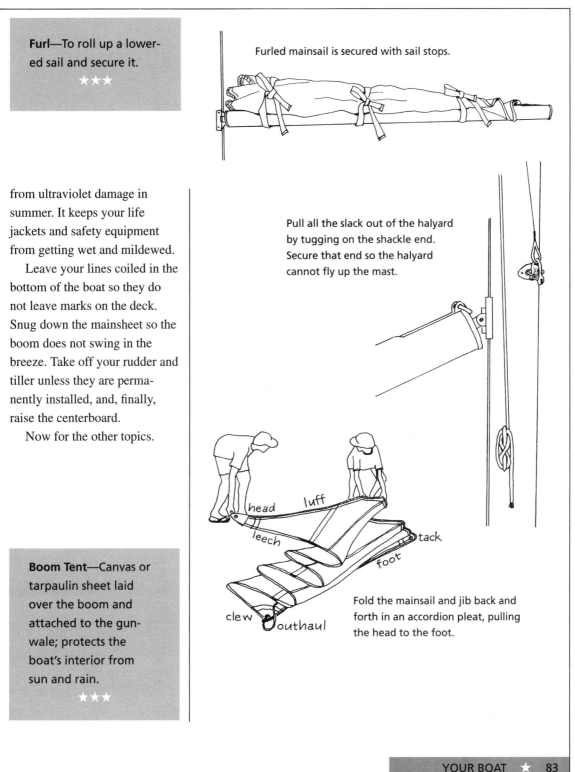

Furl—To roll up a lower-ed sail and secure it.

★★★

Furled mainsail is secured with sail stops.

from ultraviolet damage in summer. It keeps your life jackets and safety equipment from getting wet and mildewed.

Leave your lines coiled in the bottom of the boat so they do not leave marks on the deck. Snug down the mainsheet so the boom does not swing in the breeze. Take off your rudder and tiller unless they are perma-nently installed, and, finally, raise the centerboard.

Now for the other topics.

Pull all the slack out of the halyard by tugging on the shackle end. Secure that end so the halyard cannot fly up the mast.

head · luff · leech · tack · foot · clew · outhaul

Boom Tent—Canvas or tarpaulin sheet laid over the boom and attached to the gun-wale; protects the boat's interior from sun and rain.

★★★

Fold the mainsail and jib back and forth in an accordion pleat, pulling the head to the foot.

TIDES AND CURRENT

Saltwater sailors need to know how tides and current can affect their course. Tides are the vertical rise and fall of water depth around the earth caused by the gravitational pulls of the moon and sun. Current is the horizontal motion of the water as it moves in and out with tidal rise and fall.

Tides vary around the world from 2 to nearly 50 feet, but depth is not a big issue for a dinghy. You can sail in just a few inches of water and not run aground if you pull up your centerboard. Current, on the other hand, is important to keep in mind. Sometimes, especially at the mouths of big bays, currents can be quite rapid—faster than a small boat can sail. Many sailors have looked over at the shore to find that, even though sailing fast and hard, they were actually slipping backward.

You'll find tidal currents in coastal bays, rivers, and oceans.

A closed body of water such as a reservoir or a small lake has no tides. It may have tricky currents, though, caused by strong breezes churning up the water.

If the current is flowing away from your home port, it will be easy for you to get out for the day. Coming home may be more difficult, unless you have timed your return to "ride" the incoming tide, about six hours and twelve minutes later (the gap between most high and low tides).

Water flowing toward the shore or upstream is called **flood** current; water running away from the shore or downstream is **ebb** current. As the tide changes, you may see a calm on the surface—**slack water**.

You can find the times of local high and low tide from weather forecasts and local newspapers. To discover the strength of the current, you need to check with other sailors or the

Coast Guard in your area.

You will gradually develop a knack for observing current. Study the movement of water around buoys to get an idea of the current's strength and speed and direction. Notice how the water becomes choppy if the current is moving against the wind.

Ebb—Tide falling from high to low.

Flood—Tide rising from low to high.

Slack Water—Period at the turn of the tide when the water is still, neither rising nor falling.

★★★

CHARTS

Even the most experienced skippers rely on nautical charts for getting around safely in unfamiliar

waters. They are like road maps, but they also tell you what's under the water.

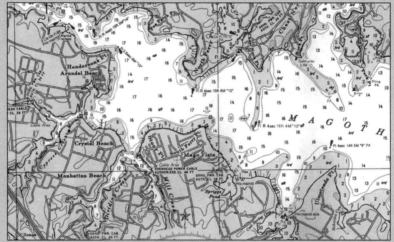

Charts help you:

- Find out where you are when you aren't sure.
- Plan the best route to get from where you are to where you want to be.

Charts tell you the depth of the water at low tide. They pinpoint sunken shipwrecks and other hidden hazards. They warn you about shallow water with rocks or mud banks where you could run aground. They show lighthouses, bridges, and prominent landmarks, such as buildings and water tanks.

Local charts often indicate buoys, which are markers that let you approach a new channel with confidence.

Buoys are red and green. If you are sailing from a large bay into a harbor, you are reckoned to be "returning." The red buoys must be on your starboard side, the green ones to port. There's a handy saying to help you remember this rule: "Red-right-returning."

In coastal waters, a chart and compass can still hold their own against the fanciest computer and satellite navigation equipment found on large yachts. And they're even more reliable when the batteries go dead.

NAUTICAL RULES OF THE ROAD

With boats going in all directions, it is necessary to have some traffic rules. They are called **Rules of the Road.** They have one purpose: to avoid collisions. They are based on a simple idea: if two boats are going to collide, one of them has to get out of the way, and both of them should know which one that is. These are the rules you live by on the water. You need to know them. There is no excuse for a collision.

As two boats approach on a collision course, which one gives way? Sailboat to sailboat, these are the rules:

- A boat on a port tack must give way to one on a starboard tack.
- When both boats are on the same tack (wind on the same side), the vessel to windward must give way to a leeward vessel (the one farthest from the wind).
- Any boat on a port tack must keep clear if its skipper is in doubt about the tack of another boat to windward.

Sailboat to powerboat: Boats under power must generally give way to boats under sail. There are three important exceptions where motorboats have the right of way:

- If a motorboat is being overtaken by a sailboat.
- If a motorboat is operating in a narrow channel and cannot maneuver easily.
- If a motorboat is too large and cumbersome to avoid a sailboat (like a tanker or a tour boat). Remember, your boat can turn on a dime, but big boats have a wide turning circle. If it is easier for you to get out of the way, you should.

The Rules of the Road have their own language. The boat with the right of way is known as the privileged or "stand on" vessel because it must "stand on" course. The boat that must change course is the burdened or "give-way" vessel.

Even when you have the right of way, you must take action to avoid a collision if another boat fails to give way. Many small motorboat operators just don't know the Rules of the Road, so keep an eye on boats around you. When coming about, be careful that your change of course does not put you across someone else's bow. If someone seems to be all over the place, steer clear.

Rules of the Road—
The nautical safety regulations that govern the movement of boats; determines who has the right of way in a meeting between two or more boats.

★★★

WIND

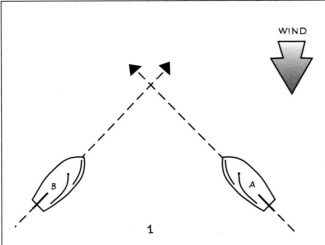

1

These boats are on opposite tacks. If one of them does not get out of the way, they will collide. Boat A is on a starboard tack with the wind coming over the starboard side. Boat B is on a port tack. Boat A has the right of way.

2

Boat A is the leeward boat because it is farther away from the wind. Boat B is windward because it is closer to the wind. Boat A has the right of way.

3

Boat A is moving more slowly than Boat B. Boat B is overtaking from behind. Boat A has the right of way. An overtaking boat does not have any rights.

"WHAT KIND OF BOAT IS THAT?"

The more you sail, the more interesting other types of boats out on the water become. There are sailboats of all shapes and sizes. This chapter will help you to recognize those you are most likely to see.

We have been talking about small boats with two triangular sails and one mast. Any boat with one mast is a **sloop**, **catboat**, or **cutter**. The International 420, which is popular for racing, is a sloop.

A catboat has just a mainsail and no jib, and the mast is up near the bow. The catboat's mainsail can be triangular (Marconi rigged) or four-sided with a **gaff**. The gaff is a small boom at the top of the sail and the boat is called **gaff rigged**. The Laser and Sunfish are catboats with triangular sails.

A cutter has one mainsail but may have two sails forward of the mast called **headsails**.

Another style of four-sided sail has an angled **spar,** called a

sprit, halfway up the mast. This rig is known as a **spritsail**, and you'll find it on the Optimist Pram and some traditional small craft such as dories and Whitehalls. Many sailing programs use Optimists for beginners.

You will see boats with more than one mast. Two or more masts means the boat is a **ketch**, a **yawl**, or a **schooner**.

- A ketch has two masts, with the smaller one aft of the larger one and the helm aft of both of them.
- A yawl has two masts, with the smaller one aft of the mainmast and also aft of the helm.
- A schooner has two or more masts, with the shorter ones forward of the mainmast.

You sometimes still see square-rigged boats similar to the ships Columbus sailed (see drawing on page 47). The many sails are

actually rectangles, not squares, and they hang from booms called **yards.** Square-riggers cannot sail as close to the wind as dinghies because it is more difficult to set their sails at an angle.

Catboat—A boat with one mast and no headsail.

Cutter—A sailboat with two headsails and one mast mounted approximately amidships.

Headsail—A sail set forward of the mast (like a jib).

Sloop—A boat with one mast, one headsail, and a mainsail.

Yard—A horizontal spar that supports a square-sail.

★★★

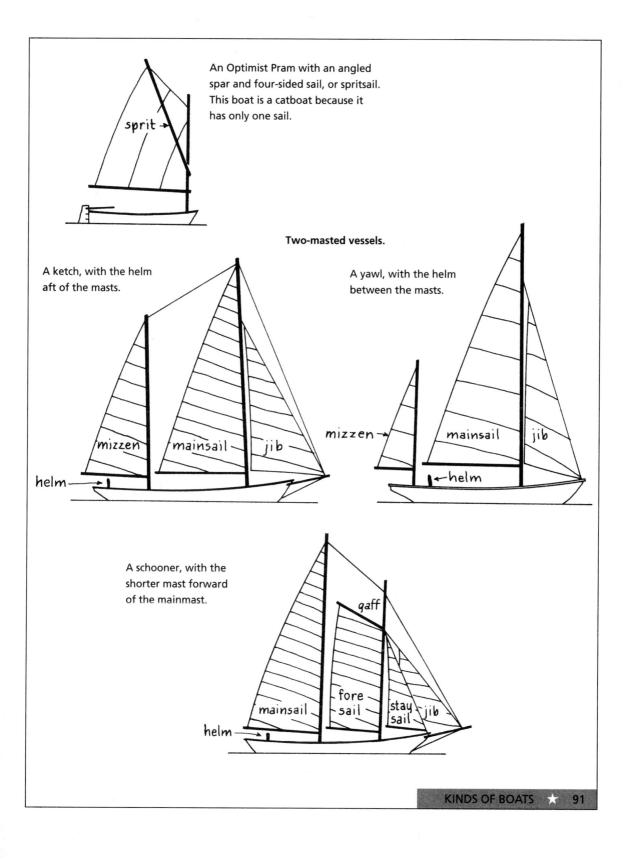

An Optimist Pram with an angled spar and four-sided sail, or spritsail. This boat is a catboat because it has only one sail.

sprit →

Two-masted vessels.

A ketch, with the helm aft of the masts.

A yawl, with the helm between the masts.

mizzen   mainsail   jib

helm

mizzen →   mainsail   jib

←helm

A schooner, with the shorter mast forward of the mainmast.

gaff

mainsail   fore sail   stay sail   jib

helm

MODERN SAILING

WHAT NEXT?

The materials used in making sails, masts, and boats are always being improved to make vessels lighter, faster, and safer. Boat designs change constantly for the same reasons.

Sails of Mylar and Kevlar, for example, are smoother, stronger, and shinier than canvas or nylon. They assist the airfoil effect and help the boat to go faster. Some masts today are made of carbon fiber to be light and strong.

You will see flat decks called **flush decks.** They have a smooth, aerodynamic design to cut down wind resistance and give the boat more speed. They can also accommodate large crews scrambling around during a race.

On bigger boats, you will see sophisticated winches and special devices for trimming sails. A growing number of oceangoing boats use computers to navigate by taking satellite readings to find their position.

As you spend more time on the water, your sailing skills will develop. You will want to move forward and seek new challenges.

If you or your family have a boat, you'll have the chance to sail regularly. If not, there are many programs that provide boats. Camps and yacht clubs often run programs for new skippers. Some of these programs teach racing as a way for you to improve your skills. Whether you sail competitively or just for the pure pleasure of being out on the water, you'll have a lifelong sport.

The most important part of sailing is making the effort and loving it. Get outside, get on the water, and find the people who can help you make your sailing experience meaningful and fun.

Sailors are lucky because their fuel—the wind—is free. It may die down at times, but it always returns and is endlessly renewable.

It all starts with the information in this book. You can go as far as your interest takes you. *Let* it take you. And let it bring you home. Maybe just for a summer of fun in a dinghy on a stretch of water near your home. Maybe on a solo transatlantic crossing. Maybe to the Olympic sailing team. Whatever you decide, happy sailing.

Flush Deck—A top deck the same height as the gunwale.
★★★

APPENDIX
TRAILERING

PUTTING UP THE MAST

If you trailer your boat to the water, you will need to raise your mast each time you sail. Leave the shrouds and backstay (if so equipped) attached to the mast and the boat. Only unhook the forestay. Tie down the stays and shrouds for the journey so they do not tangle.

Two people are needed to raise the mast. One holds the mast up, while the other fastens the forestay to a fitting on the bow.

LAUNCHING

Small boats are often kept on trailers, which are easy to roll in and out of the water. You may decide to rig while your boat is on the trailer. If you do, wait until the boat has been pushed into the water and secured by the bow line before you raise the sails.

If you keep your boat on a trailer, put the centerboard in the up position for storing.

PUTTING THE BOAT BACK ON THE TRAILER

If you are pulling the boat onto a trailer, let the boat ride in a few inches of water. Back the trailer down to the boat and float the boat on. Tie the boat's bow line to the hook on the trailer. Pull the loaded trailer out of the water. You may have a crank handle to wind up the bow line and drag the boat onto the trailer. You will probably have a strap that hooks onto the sides of the trailer and goes over the boat. Pull that tight before heading home. Secure all loose gear or put it in the car. If you use a canvas cover, tie it down tightly for travel on the road.

GLOSSARY/INDEX

A review of sailing terms used in this book. You'll also find them as labels on the illustrations or listed with a definition on the page where they first appear. The numbers in parentheses indicate where a term or concept is discussed.

Abeam—At right angles to the side of the boat. (51)

Aft—Toward the stern or back of the boat. (3, 4)

Airfoil—The lifting effect created when air moves at different speeds across both sides of a curved surface. (46–48, 52, 92)

Aloft—Up. (9)

Amidships—The middle of the boat, from side to side or from front to back. (57)

Anchor—A heavy metal object used to hold a boat in place when it is not at a dock or mooring buoy. (25, 74–75, 76, 81)

Anchor rode—A line for the anchor. (25, 74–75)

Backstay—A cable supporting the mast; runs from the stern to the top of the mast. (93)

Bail—To remove water from a boat using a scoop or bucket called a *bailer*. (24, 69)

Bare Poles—Sailing without sails set, generally in a heavy wind. (73, 75, 79)

Battens—Flat pieces of wood or fiberglass used to flatten the leech edge of a sail. (5, 12, 42)

Beam—The widest part of the boat. (3)

Beam Reach—A point of sail with the wind coming directly over the side of the boat. (51–52, 54, 55, 60, 65, 69)

Bearing—The direction of one object from another, measured in degrees from north, or measured relative to the boat's center-line. (26)

Beat (to Windward)—To sail close to the wind to reach a place lying upwind of you. (62–63)

Bend On—To fasten sails to a boat. (6–8, 19–20)

Block—The nautical term for a pulley. (7, 11)

Boltrope—Reinforcing rope sewn along the foot of a sail. (5, 6–7, 19)

Boom—A spar running at a right angle from the mast to hold the foot of a sail. (3, 6–8, 32, 36, 51–52, 57–59, 60–61, 64, 74, 79)

Boom Tent—A canvas or plastic sheet laid over the boom and attached to the gunwale; protects the boat's interior from sun and rain. (82–83)

Bow (pronounced as in a dog's bark, not as in "bow and arrow")—the front end of a boat. (2, 3)

Bowline (pronounced 'bō-lun)—This strong knot creates a loop in the end of a line that doesn't slip and is easy to untie. (81)

Broad Reach—A point of sail between a beam reach and running, between 90 and 180 degrees away from the wind. (53, 54, 60, 65)

Bungee Cord—Stretchy, elastic line. (16)

Cam Cleat—A spring-loaded clamp for securing the mainsheet or jibsheets. (15, 42)

Capsize—To turn over. (16, 66, 68–69, 76)

Cast Off—To untie from a dock or mooring. (36, 38)

Catboat—A boat with one mast and no headsail. (90–91)

Centerboard—A pivoting board that prevents a boat from sliding sideways (called *leeway*). (2–3, 16–18, 19, 40–41, 48, 68–69, 75, 81, 83, 93)

Centerboard Trunk—Housing for the centerboard. (16–17)

Clam Cleat—A clamp with ridges for securing the mainsheet or jibsheets. (15)

Cleat Hitch—Secures line to a horn cleat. (8–9, 11–12, 19)

Clew—The aft lower corner of a sail. (4–5, 7, 8, 19, 82)

Close Hauled—A point of sail with the wind coming from just forward of the bow; sailing as close to the wind as possible. (51–52, 54, 55, 62–63, 64–65, 80)

Close Reach—A point of sail between close hauled and beam reach; between 45 and 90 degrees to the wind. (53, 54, 64–65, 80)

Cockpit—The area inside the hull where the captain and crew operate. (3)

Come About—To turn the boat to the opposite tack by putting the bow through the wind. (41, 57–59, 60, 62, 64, 70–71)

Compass (hand-bearing)—A magnetic device that indicates the direction of magnetic north. (25, 26, 40, 76, 85)

Correct—To bring the boat on course with slight movements of the tiller. (40–41, 64)

Cutter—A sailboat with two headsails and one mast mounted approximately amidships. (90)

Daggerboard—A centerboard that slides vertically through a slot in the hull to prevent it from slipping sideways (see **Centerboard**). (16–17, 68)

Deck—The flat surface area of a boat, like a floor at home. (3, 92)

Dinghy—A small open boat. (4)

Downwind—Sailing with the wind behind on a broad reach or a run. (46–47, 52–55, 60, 62, 79)

Ease Off—To let out. (8)

Ebb—Tide falling from high to low. (84)

Fairlead—A pulley or ring used to direct sheets or other lines. (14, 19)

Fall Off—To move the bow away from the wind. (32, 34, 54)

Flood—Tide rising from low to high. (84)

Flush Deck—A top deck the same height as the gunwale. (92)

Fore and Aft—Running from front to back or back to front. (4)

Foot—The bottom edge of the sail, parallel to the deck. (4–5, 7, 19, 82–83)

Foresail (pronounced ˈfor-sul)—The forwardmost sail on a boat. (91)

Forestay—Cable supporting the mast, running from the bow to the top of the mast. (3, 13, 17, 93)

Forward—Toward the bow or front of a boat. (3, 4)

Foul-Weather Gear—Clothing that protects against wind and rain. (22, 27)

Furl—To roll up a lowered sail and secure it. (74, 82–83)

Gaff—A spar that supports the head of a four-sided fore-and-aft sail. (90–91)

Gaff-rigged—A boat with a four-sided sail whose head is held up by a gaff. (90)

Gooseneck—A fexible fitting that holds the boom to the mast. (6, 20, 74)

Grommet—A metal ring in a sail through which lines or shackles can pass. (6, 7, 11, 13)

Gunwale (pronounced ˈgun-nel)—The top edge of the side of the hull. (3)

Gudgeon—An eyed fitting on the stern of the boat that holds the rudder. (16)

Halyard—A line used to hoist sails. (9–12, 14, 19–20, 74, 81, 82–83)

Head—The top corner of a sail. (4–5, 10–11, 82–83)

Headboard—Plastic or metal reinforcement at the head of a sail. (10)

Heading—The direction your boat is going. (50)

Headsail—A sail set forward of the mast (like a jib). (90)

Head Up—To move the bow toward the wind. (54, 70, 75, 78)

Heave To (hove to)—To set the sails and the rudder so the boat does not sail. You do this when you want to hold your position. (73, 74, 75, 76)

Heel—Leaning of the boat to one side in response to the wind. (66, 68, 75)

Helm—The tiller or wheel that controls the rudder (see **Tiller**). (38, 74, 91)

Hike—To balance a heeling boat with body weight. (66)

Hiking Strap—A fore-and-aft strap that holds your feet as you lean out over the side to balance the boat in heavy air. (66)

Horn Cleat—A horn-shaped metal fitting bolted to a boat or dock; used to secure lines. (8, 15)

Hull—The main body of a boat. (2–3)

In Irons—When the bow is in the no-sail zone, the sails are luffing, and the boat isn't moving forward. (54)

Jam Cleat—Similar to a horn cleat, but with a pinched end that secures a line on one wraparound. (15, 59, 78)

Jib (rhymes with bib)—A headsail set forward of the mast. (3, 4, 13–14, 19, 42–44, 54, 57–59, 60, 74, 75, 82, 91)

Jibe—To turn around by putting the stern of a boat through the wind. (41, 57, 60–63, 64, 68, 70–71)

Jib Hanks—Metal snaps that attach the jib to the forestay. (13, 19)

Jibheaded—A boat with triangular sails (also called *Marconi*). (52)

Jibsheet—A line used to pull the jib in or let it out. (3, 13–14, 19, 42–43, 59, 60-61, 69, 75, 81, 82)

Keel—A fore-and-aft extension below the boat that prevents the boat from slipping sideways. (2–3, 16, 40)

Ketch—A boat with two masts, with the forward mast being the larger, or mainmast. The helm is aft of both masts. (90–91)

Leech—The aft and longest edge of a triangular sail. (4–5, 12, 13)

Leeward (pronounced 'loo-ard)—The direction away from the wind. (36–37, 38, 57–59, 70–71, 74, 86–87)

Leeway—Sideways motion of a boat; caused by wind pressure. (16–18)

Line—Rope, to sailors. (9, 23)

Loose-footed—A sail secured to a boom only at the tack and the clew. (7)

Luff—(**1**) The forward edge of triangular sail. (4–5, 11, 13, 19, 46, 82–83) (**2**) Rippling or flapping at the forward edge of a sail. (6, 32, 36, 42–43, 48, 54, 59, 60, 68, 70–71, 74, 79, 80) (**3**) Luff (Up)— To spill wind. (66, 68, 70–71, 74, 79, 80)

Luff Point—Moment at which a sail is let out too far and begins to ripple at the forward edge. (42–43, 51–52, 54, 59)

Magnetic North—The point near the North Pole toward which the needle of a compass is drawn. (26)

Mainmast—The tallest mast. (90–91)

Mainsail (pronounced 'main-sul)—The largest sail on the mainmast. (3, 4, 6–12, 19, 42–44, 45, 57–59, 60–61, 74, 75, 79, 82–83, 91)

Mainsheet—A line used to pull the mainsail in or let it out. (3, 11, 19, 42, 59, 60–61, 64, 66, 68, 69, 74, 75, 79, 81, 83)

Make Fast—To secure a line by tying a knot or a hitch. (8)

Marconi—A boat with triangular sails (also called *jibheaded*). (52, 90)

Marline (pronounced 'mar-lun)—Tarred twine. (24)

Marlinspike—A pointed tool for splicing line and undoing knots. (24)

Mast—A tall spar that holds up the sails. (2–3, 69, 90–91, 92, 93)

Mizzen(mast)—The after and shorter mast on a ketch or a yawl. (91)

Mizzen—The small sail on the mizzenmast. (91)

Mooring—An anchored float to tie up to. (32–34, 78)

No-Sail Zone—A pie-slice–shaped area 45 degrees on either side of the wind's direction. (32–34, 36, 48, 50–55, 57–59, 60–62, 64–65, 69, 78, 79–80)

Outhaul—A short line at the clew corner of a mainsail; used to secure the foot. (7–8)

Peak—The after upper corner of a four-sided sail. (90–91)

Pennant—(**1**) A line used to raise or lower a centerboard. (16–17) (**2**) A line used to tie a boat to a mooring. (78)

Pintle—A pin on the rudder that slides into a fitting on the stern called a *gudgeon*. (16)

water is still, neither rising nor falling. (84)

Sloop—A boat with one mast, one headsail, and a mainsail. (90–91)

Spar—The nautical term for a mast, boom, or gaff. (90)

Sprit—A spar that runs diagonally from near the tack to extend the peak of a four-sided fore-and-aft sail. (90–91)

Spritsail (pronounced 'sprit-sul)—A four-sided sail with the peak extended by a sprit. (90–91)

Stall—When a sail has lost its wind and no longer acts as an airfoil. You might stall a sail to slow down. (42, 64)

Starboard—The right side of a boat when you are looking forward. (3, 9, 86)

Stays—Wire cables that hold up the mast, running fore and aft (see **Backstay, Forestay**). (2, 93)

Staysail (pronounced 'stay-sul)—A triangular headsail attached to a stay. (91)

Stern—The back end of a boat. (2, 3, 40–41)

Stopper Knot—A knot that prevents line from slipping through an opening. (14–15, 19)

Stow—To put away. (9)

Tack—(**1**) The forward lower corner of sail. (4–5, 6, 8, 19–20, 82) (**2**) The direction of the wind on sails (as in port tack or starboard tack). (36–37, 50–52, 57, 86–87) (**3**) To change tacks back and forth on a close-hauled point of sail to move toward the wind. (41, 57–59, 60, 62–63, 64)

Tack Pin—A metal peg that secures the tack corner of the mainsail to the boom. (6, 7, 19)

Telltale—Yarn tied to the shroud to indicate wind direction. (30–31, 37, 55)

Thwart—A seat that extends across the cockpit. (66)

Tiller—A long handle attached to the rudder for steering a boat. (2, 3, 16, 38, 40–41, 42–43, 54, 57–59, 60–61, 64, 74, 79, 83)

Timber Hitch—A series of loops that can come undone with one pull on the end of the sheet. (79)

Transom—The flattened back end of a boat; a dinghy's rudder is usually mounted here. (16)

Trim—To adjust the sails to make the most of the wind. (42–43, 50–55, 59, 92)

Underway—When the boat is moving and under control. (3, 30)

Way—Momentum or speed in sailing. (57)

Well—A slot through which the centerboard or daggerboard fits. (16–17)

Winch—A geared drum that makes it easier to pull in lines. (26, 44, 59, 92)

Windward—The direction the wind is coming from. (36–37, 38, 59, 62–63, 86–87)

Yard—A horizontal spar that supports a squaresail. (90)

Yawl—A boat with two masts. The forwardmost mast is the mainmast. The aftermost mast, or mizzen, is aft of the helm. (90–91)